CRIPPLED

CRIPPLED

*Austerity and the Demonization
of Disabled People*

Second Edition

Frances Ryan

VERSO

This edition first published by Verso 2020
First published by Verso 2019
© Frances Ryan 2019, 2020

1 3 5 7 9 10 8 6 4 2

Verso
UK: 6 Meard Street, London W1F 0EG
US: 20 Jay Street, Suite 1010, Brooklyn, NY 11201
versobooks.com

Verso is the imprint of New Left Books

ISBN-13: 978-1-78873-956-6
ISBN-13: 978-1-78663-789-5 (UK EBK)
ISBN-13: 978-1-78663-790-1 (US EBK)

British Library Cataloguing in Publication Data
A catalogue record for this book is available from the British Library

The Library of Congress Has Cataloged the First Edition as Follows:

Names: Ryan, Frances, author.
Title: Crippled : austerity and the demonization of disabled people / Frances
  Ryan.
Description: Brooklyn : Verso, 2019.
Identifiers: LCCN 2019007281| ISBN 9781786637888 (paperback) | ISBN
  9781786637895 (UK ebk) | ISBN 9781786637901 (US ebk)
Subjects: LCSH: People with disabilities – Government policy – Great Britain. |
  People with disabilities – Services for – Great Britain. | BISAC: POLITICAL
  SCIENCE / History & Theory. | POLITICAL SCIENCE / Civics & Citizenship.
Classification: LCC HV1559.G7 R93 2019 | DDC 362.4/04560941 – dc23
LC record available at https://lccn.loc.gov/2019007281

Typeset in Adobe Garamond Pro by Hewer Text UK Ltd, Edinburgh
Printed and bound by CPI roup (UK) Ltd, Croydon CR0 4YY

For Mum, Dad, and Kate

Contents

Acknowledgements   ix

Introduction   1

  1 Poverty   11

  2 Work   39

  3 Independence   73

  4 Housing   105

  5 Women   137

  6 Children   169

Conclusion   191

Afterword: A Fairer Society in the Age of
  Coronavirus   201

Notes   211

Help and Resources   233

Index   237

Acknowledgements

The book would not have happened without my editor at Verso, Leo Hollis, whose confidence in me helped transform a notebook of ideas into a book on a shelf. My agent, Diana Beaumont, has offered invaluable support throughout. I'm also very grateful to the K Blundell Trust and the Society of Authors for their grant and faith in the project.

A number of experts have contributed helpful advice, including Ellen Clifford and Disabled People against Cuts, Ben Baumberg Geiger, Michelle Cardno at Fightback4Justice, and many more. Charities such as Contact, Scope, Leonard Cheshire, Action for Children, Changing Lives, the Joseph Rowntree Foundation, DeafHope, SafeLives and Refuge have similarly generously offered their time to be interviewed, track down sources, or bat around ideas.

I have been very lucky to have the support of family and friends who, in multiple ways, helped me complete this book at a challenging time – in particular Dave Drew, Aisling Wootten, Marie Staniforth, Sarah Raddon Jackson, Helen McCulloch and Sarah

Monk. As ever, my love and thanks for everything to Mum, Dad, and sister, Kate.

This book was in many ways the accumulation of six years' work covering disability and austerity, started long before I envisaged writing a book or there being an interest in publishing it. In light of that, thank you to the editors and colleagues who over the years have offered anything from early commissions or advice to the encouragement that helped me get here – in particular, Kira Cochrane, Amelia Gentleman, Alison Benjamin, Patrick Butler and Helen Lewis.

It was with more than a little irony that, just as I embarked upon writing a book about disability, my own disability took a considerable downturn. Writing became impossible for much of the time and, when possible, was slow and stagnated. There were times when I did not know if I'd physically be able to get this book out. And yet I was incredibly fortunate. I had a family that meant I never needed to worry about keeping a roof over my head and a flexible job that meant I could work – and therefore earn a wage – from my bed. Countless others do not. It is here that my appreciation for the welfare state is only encouraged. To have a safety net to protect us when we are sick is the most precious of things and a sign of civilization we shall surely miss if it's gone.

Since I began working on this subject in 2012, many hundreds of disabled people have taken the time to write to me about their experiences. These tweets, letters and emails were fundamental in shaping the work that followed. Above anyone, I would like to thank the disabled people who agreed to be interviewed for this book. I am deeply aware how exposing and difficult it often was to relay some of the most intimate parts of their lives, and the bravery it took to share that publicly. I thank them for their trust and hope this book does them justice.

Introduction

In the closing stages of 2015, it emerged the United Nations was quietly carrying out an inquiry into state-level violations of disabled people's human rights. It was the first of its kind: a secret investigation into the harm a government was allegedly inflicting on its disabled citizens. Initial reports included some distressing accounts from disabled people and their families. The UN insisted on conducting proceedings in private, stating that confidentiality was necessary to 'protect witnesses' and to 'secure the co-operation of the host country'.[1]

It would be easy to assume that the 'host country' in question was an undemocratic regime with a dire record on human rights or perhaps a developing nation without the rich economy needed to provide a social safety net. In fact, it was Britain.

Fast-forward two years to 2017 and the United Nations was releasing an unprecedented judgement: the conditions for disabled people in Britain were tantamount to a 'human catastrophe'.[2] In the succeeding months, the UN declared the British state was failing in its duties towards its disabled citizens in everything from housing and employment to education and social security.[3] Somehow, one of the wealthiest nations on earth – and with it, arguably the most pioneering welfare system in the Western world – was now receiving international condemnation for its treatment of disabled people.

I grew up in a Britain that said life was going to be full of promise for disabled people like me. In the 1990s, grim words like 'crippled' and 'retarded' were no longer part of everyday speech. Disability was still often missing from the media and positions of power but – unlike the many generations before me – I could say I lived in a country where ordinary disabled people were no longer hidden from sight. Moreover, the charity tins that until recently had symbolized the scraps handed out to disabled citizens were now accompanied by rights. These reached from the groundbreaking disability civil rights law of my childhood to the welfare state's tailor-made benefits and services for disabled people.

In the days after the London Olympics 2012, the Paralympics became the poster child for this sense of optimism. A focus of national pride, the event was not only pitched as a demonstration of what disabled people could achieve when given the chance, but a vehicle for Britain to assert its position as a global leader for disability on the world stage. At the launch of the games, Prime Minister David Cameron claimed he was proud that Britain was 'a trailblazer for disability rights'.[4] In reality, only a few months earlier, Cameron and colleagues had been setting in motion a political agenda that ushered in the unprecedented demolition of

Britain's safety net for disabled people and, in doing so, rolled back hard-won disability rights by decades.

From its election as part of a coalition government in 2010, the British Conservative Party under David Cameron oversaw a programme of cuts not seen since the 1920s. Framed as a necessary response to the global economic crash, it launched what turned out to be Britain's long-term austerity project: hollowing out 'welfare', public services and local council budgets.

While then chancellor George Osborne promised we were 'all in it together', in fact it was disabled people who were targeted to take the greatest hit, with tens of billions of pounds being pulled from everything from disability benefits to housing to social care provision.[5] The Centre for Welfare Reform calculated in 2013 that disabled people would endure nine times the burden of cuts compared to the average citizen, with people with the most severe disabilities being hit a staggering nineteen times harder.[6] A global recession caused by bankers and stoked by right-wing politicians was set to punish paraplegics and cancer patients.

This did not come about by accident but rather was a deliberate attack on disabled people in Britain. In a climate of disenfranchisement, squeezed wages and growing individualism, disabled people became Britain's new favourite target. Ministers spoke freely about the 'work-shy' long-term sick exploiting hard-working taxpayers. Television shows openly mocked working-class sick and disabled families. Newspapers began to eagerly hunt out examples of so-called scrounging disabled people.

The scapegoating of the disabled had become a respectable, mainstream part of British culture. In 2012, the *Sun* launched a campaign to 'Beat the Cheat', even setting up its own national benefit-fraud hotline and calling on 'patriotic Brits' to 'name and shame fiddling scroungers' in their areas.[7] Such editorials were not throwaway fringe reporting but consistently supported by those at the heart of government. When in 2014 the *Daily Express* listed 'a rogues gallery of 10 of the most outrageous con artists' on benefits, then welfare chief Iain Duncan Smith was happy to provide a sound bite for the baiting headline: 'We'll root out the benefits cheats who pretend to be ill for money.'[8]

The message in all of this was simple and effective. It was not a global economic crash that had caused a recession but the so-called bloated welfare bill covering the needs of supposedly disabled people. It was not high private rents, insecure jobs or low wages that was the root of people's problems but their disabled neighbour living an easy life on benefits.

Demonizing people on the bottom rung of society has been a method of reinforcing the status quo through the ages. This has long particularly been the case during times of economic crisis, where minorities and marginalized groups become scapegoats of those in power. But what was unique about the scapegoating of disabled people post-2010 was that the group now being sacrificed was the very people society had always promised to protect.

Over the past couple of decades, we have got used to politicians describing Britain as a country that has always exuded a sense of fairness and decency. And the treatment of Britain's disabled citizens is in many ways at the heart of this. We have all heard the phrase 'the mark of a civilized society is how it treats its most vulnerable citizens'. It is an idiom long-used to articulate Britain's apparent caring attitude to disabled people. In many ways, providing a 'safety net' for citizens struggling with poor health is central to Britain's very identity of decency and fairness – one that comes with the in-built claim that even in 'tough economic times' disabled people would always have a safety net to rely on.

This book will show not only that this is rose-tinted revisionism of Britain's long-troubled relationship with disability, but also that the austerity era has seen those in power abandon even a pretence of duty to disabled citizens and brutally turn against them. Disabled people – once a source of compassion and care – had become an object of suspicion, demonization and contempt. It was official: under austerity, the one group in society who had been supposedly untouchable was now said to be unaffordable.

As ministers and much of the media spoke of the bloated disability bill, over the course of six years I began to talk daily to the disabled people living behind the rhetoric.

Each was very different: some had left school in their teens, while others had held traditionally middle-class jobs until bad health hit; some were lifelong Labour voters, others had no interest in politics at all; some were born disabled, while others developed mental health problems or chronic illness in later life. But all had something in common: post-2010, each was now living in the sort of hardship they had never imagined possible.

Jimbob was one of them. I first spoke to the sixty-eight-year-old in the freezing winter of 2017, just a few months after the general election had seen the Conservative Party returned to power. Jimbob has chronic lung disease – 'It's like trying to breathe through a straw whilst running,' he told me – as well as multiple other health problems, including bone disease, a progressive spinal condition, and fibromyalgia, a long-term dose of extreme tiredness and muscle stiffness. Jimbob had earned a wage since he was twelve – first for his dad at a garage through the 1960s and 1970s and then as an engineer – but, as he put it, 'when your health packs in, that's it'.

His two-bed flat in Ayrshire, Scotland, is built with concrete – the sort of home that has a chill running through the walls all year round and bites in the winter – and for years, disability benefits were his only way to heat it. But when the government rolled out 'tougher' social security tests in 2013, he had his support taken off him. A hundred pounds a week gone, just like that.

It means that Jimbob now lives in his bedroom. In order to afford to keep the lights on in the flat and have enough gas for the cooker – and with it, hot meals – he only heats one room. When it's necessary to move – say, to get to the toilet – Jimbob explained he's developed a '15 minute rule': he puts the heating on in the hallway, then waits a quarter of an hour to move from his bedroom to an unheated room. Otherwise, he can't physically stand it.

As we talk, Jimbob sat wrapped in a quilt for a double bed. The temperature gauge on his oven said it was ten degrees in his kitchen: barely a few degrees more than the temperature outside. That would be a tough way to live for anyone, but for Jimbob it's physically punishing. The cold air in the house aggravates his chest and makes his already painful joints throb, while his other disabilities mean he does not have the strength to keep moving to warm his body up. I asked Jimbob what it's like when he gets cold and his answer was simple: 'You feel like you're dying.'

He coughed as we talked; there were heavy-duty steroids in the flat from a recent bout of breathing problems. On the toughest days, when the cold goes through his lungs and bones, Jimbob puts his coat on, takes his dog and gets into his old Jeep. The car, he explained, has under-seat heating and he and the dog – 'my trusty companion' – sit there together. Last winter, Jimbob worked out he might be able to survive without heating in the flat if only he could get himself in a confined space. That same day, he looked out some old camping equipment and pitched it next to his sofa. There he was, huddled up inside a tent in the middle of the living room.

As I listened to Jimbob, there was a feeling that stood out perhaps more than any other. You might call it injustice; or, put another way, the feeling of someone being lied to. Before he became disabled, Jimbob believed he grew up under a welfare state that offered him a promise: if the time came when he really needed it, a safety net would be there to catch him. Not a fortune but enough to eat regular meals and put the heating on in winter. 'I used to feel as long as you did your bit, worked hard, there'd be a system [to help you],' he told me. 'Now, it feels like the system's after you. Like you're a scrounger.'

This book is, at its heart, a story about Britain's Jimbobs. What it shows is some of the reality of disabled people's existence that in recent years has been airbrushed out by a toxic mix of vilification and false promises. Through the voices of those affected, this book will show that the very safety net said to protect people in times of sickness and disability has, in fact, worked to impoverish millions and deprived hundreds of thousands of even the most basic dignities of everyday life. The scale of this is nothing less than a national scandal.

In 2018, a report by the government's equality watchdog, the Equality and Human Rights Commission (EHRC), found that one in five British people were suffering erosion of their rights because they are disabled, citing 'deeply concerning' evidence that – contrary to government claims – conditions for disabled Britons are actually getting worse.[9] Only a few months later, the EHRC released a ground-breaking report into the 'alarming backward steps' Britain had taken in its quest to achieve a more equal society in recent years, citing disabled people – far from having been protected – as one of the worst-affected groups.[10]

But this book not only seeks to serve as a corrective to the lie that the disabled – or 'society's most vulnerable' – will always be protected. It seeks to challenge the notion of vulnerability itself. One of the most pervasive and damaging myths in modern liberal societies is the idea that disabled people are 'the most vulnerable'. This is a by-product of a culture that still widely associates disability with tragedy and perpetuates an individual analysis for something that is fundamentally structural. This attitude is now so prevalent that even people on the left use this language, where well-meaning non-disabled people profess concern over how austerity is hurting 'the most vulnerable'.

Disabled people, truth be told, do not need to be vulnerable. Contrary to the cultural myths surrounding disability, it is not inevitable for people with disabilities to be afraid, desperate or isolated. Vulnerability comes when politicians choose to pull the support disabled people need in order to live dignified, fulfilling, independent lives – knowing full well the misery it will cause.

The ill-treatment of disabled people is set to be at the heart of British politics for years to come. While Theresa May announced in September 2018 that 'austerity is over',[11] billions of pounds of cuts will continue to come into force until the 2020s, while a deepening social care crisis will further disproportionately hurt people with disabilities or illnesses. Brexit, meanwhile, will test not only attitudes towards difference but what resources even a left-leaning government will be free to plug into services for disabled people.

It would be easy to believe that all of this has very little to do with you. Many of you reading this book will not be disabled. Perhaps the word 'disability' inspires your heartfelt concern yet still somehow seems something that happens to *other people*. But the belief that disability is separate from how the rest of society lives is half the battle, that comforting idea that disability could never happen to you, and that disabled people – different, 'other' – ultimately doesn't quite have something to do with how 'normal' people live.

'Othering' (even the benevolent sort) is an illusion. Disability touches many of our lives: an estimated 12 million people in Britain have some sort of disability, both visible and invisible. Millions more are unpaid carers for a loved one who's disabled or chronically ill. If we are not carers or disabled ourselves now, many of us will be at some point. But more than that, the point is, surely, that the human divide is not as clear-cut as it often appears to be: disabled people hold the same hopes, fears and values as anyone else.

This book is a rallying cry against the shrinking of the welfare state and the hardship the austerity agenda is causing disabled people. But as much, it is attitudes it hopes to challenge. After all, the dismantling of Britain's safety net for disabled people did not come out of thin air. It is a product of a society that, despite its protestations, has still not come to grips with disability.

The first step to change is by admitting the problem.

CHAPTER 1

Poverty

'When you get your social security letter it tells you on there the amount of money the government says you need to live on. But by the time you take out all my bills, I've nothing to live on,' Susan tells me from her bungalow in east London.

The fifty-eight-year-old has a range of health problems – among them a severe spinal condition that means for the last twenty years she's needed a wheelchair. A serious bowel condition, on top of what her consultants suspect is multiple sclerosis, brings chronic pain and shortened breaths. She struggles when her body's too weak to get out of bed, let alone hold down a job. Money has been tight since having to leave work as a bookkeeper in the 1990s. However, it is the wave of cuts to disability support, ushered in by David Cameron's coalition government over the spring of 2013, that has pushed her over the edge.

Susan's second bedroom is filled with a large oxygen cylinder, boxes of heavy-duty painkillers, and a bed for a carer when she's too ill to cope alone. The room now costs her twelve pounds a week due to the bedroom tax, the policy that penalizes social housing tenants for 'under-occupying' their homes. Council tax now takes another twelve pounds a month. Like thousands of disabled people in poverty, Susan used to be exempt from this charge but the cuts to council tax support has seen her have to pay for the first time.

Her care bill takes another chunk. Susan has a carer for thirty-seven hours a week but since local council cuts came in a few years back, she has to find fifty-seven pounds a week out of her own money for it. Her incontinence pads, a necessity with her bowel condition, used to be paid for by her health authority but Susan now has to cover the ten pounds a week herself. Another four pounds a week goes on a network alarm to hang around her neck. She has been found unconscious and out of her wheelchair before, but if she doesn't have the money, the emergency button will get shut off.

I first spoke to Susan in the autumn of 2013, just after the first round of austerity measures came into force. By that time, after only six months of social security cuts, her gas and electricity were already in arrears. She could not afford to put her heating on and had stopped using her oven. As her benefits shrank, she was scared to run up any bills. In the day, she used hot-water bottles and blankets to keep warm. By 7 p.m., as the cold crept in, she was huddled up in bed with her dog.

I went back to see her four years later in the summer of 2017, only a few weeks after Theresa May's Conservatives returned to power. In Susan's own words, life had become 'unbearable'. 'Year by year, it's getting worse.' As utility bills, food prices and inflation have risen in recent years, her reduced benefits were stretched to breaking point. She stopped going out socially, 'even to the pictures': she can't afford the taxi fare there – a bus is no good when you faint in your wheelchair – and besides, she explained, she hasn't got money for the cup of tea when she gets there. Her greatest extravagance is using the electricity to run her nebulizer four times a day to help her breathe.

Susan's two-bed bungalow is covered with the signs of her ill health: an electric wheelchair, grab rails and a bathing chair on wheels in the bathroom, and 'two-handled' mugs for her shaking hands. But it's the empty cupboards that stand out. Nowadays, she can rarely afford food. Her bowel condition means she can't safely eat solids or absorb vitamins naturally and needs specialist meals: a chemically pureed food her body can digest easily. But it's £3.50 a go. Two years ago, she stopped buying it completely: since the benefit cuts have come in, she just doesn't have the money any more. 'My doctor's telling me I need a certain diet but the government means I can't afford it.'

Instead, she lives off cereal. Susan's done the sums. A box is a couple of pounds. Porridge bulks out her stomach. She can't eat meat because of her digestive condition but the alternatives may as well be pieces of gold. 'Have you seen the price of fish lately? It's a luxury.' The only way she could afford it, she says, is if she won the lottery. 'And I can't afford that now. They've doubled the price of a ticket. Two pounds is a box of cereal.'

Susan's lost four kilos in the five years since her benefits were cut and her weight is still dropping. 'I'm starving,' she says. 'Starving.'

∽

This is what it is to be disabled in modern Britain. In one of the richest societies in history, disabled people are living in near-Dickensian levels of hardship. It would be comforting to believe Susan was a rare case – an upsetting but ultimately token incident. Describe it to the average government minister and they would likely utter words of muted outrage – that what's happening to one woman in the front room of an east London flat is sad but ultimately a blip in Britain's otherwise fair and humane system. But talk to a local charity gifting a food hamper to a dad with Parkinson's or a welfare rights adviser buried in benefit appeals forms from desperate clients – or, indeed, listen to people like Susan themselves – and such accounts of precarity are the tip of the iceberg.

Research by the Joseph Rowntree Foundation (JRF) shows that 4 million disabled adults are now living below the breadline in 2018.[1] To get a picture of the scale of this, that number accounts for over a third of all adults in poverty in the country.[2] One in five disabled people in Britain are currently in food poverty, according to Scope research in 2017,[3] which means routinely skipping meals or going without essential nutrients. The same study found one in six disabled people now report having to wear a coat indoors.[4] They're cold but they can't afford to put the heating on.

In 2017, the Equality and Human Rights Commission (EHRC) released a study detailing what can only be described as an epidemic of disability poverty in Britain. It found that even having a disabled loved one is enough to push a whole family into hardship: almost six in ten families that include a disabled person are currently living without even basic necessities, such as food or shelter.[5] That's twice as many as the total population.

This would be bad enough but most calculations of the number of disabled people in poverty may actually be under-estimates, as few take into consideration the extra costs of disability – that is, the fact that, unlike others, disabled people often have to stretch their income to pay not just for food, utilities and rent, but also for anything from a wheel-chair to extra heating in the winter. In 2018, for the first time, as well as looking at incomes, the Social Metrics Commission measured poverty in a way that took into account what it called the 'inescapable costs' of disability. It found that more than half of families living below the bread-line now contain at least one person with a disability.[6]

Poverty – and with it, inequality – for disabled people is not a fresh stain on Britain. In the nineteenth century, as the Poor Law set out to reduce the so-called financial drain of the poor, destitute disabled people were routinely housed in the squalor of the workhouses, while others – dubbed 'idiots' and 'lunatics' – were put in pauper asylums. At a time in which the state was deemed to have no duty of care to its disabled citizens, disabled people were forced to beg in the street or go cap in hand to growing charitable organizations, such as the tellingly named 'Guild of the Brave Poor Things'.

As I grew up with a disability in the 1990s, this sort of treatment felt quite alien; a dark chapter for the history books. But even in the boom of New Labour, despite undeniable vast progress on a number of measures, millions of disabled people, supposedly protected by the modern welfare state, were still living in poverty. In 2005, three out of ten disabled adults of working age were below the breadline, according to the Joseph Rowntree Foundation.[7] That's almost a third of disabled people in the country living in day-to-day hardship.

Over the next decade, this disability inequality has remained firmly in place: as of 2015–16, poverty rates for disabled and non-disabled households stayed almost static (31 per cent and 19 per cent respectively).[8]

It would be grim enough that, as each year has passed, the UK has made next to no progress on lifting disabled people out of poverty. Or that far from uniquely being 'protected' by the British state, the very citizens most in need have, for decades, actually been more likely to be in poverty than anyone else. But as Susan's empty cupboards show, when it comes to our government's treatment of disabled people, we are at a point that's more shameful still. Rather than the state struggling to provide a safety net for people with disabilities, it's now actively pushing them further into poverty itself.

In the wake of the 2008 financial crash, David Cameron and colleagues set upon an unprecedented wave of austerity in which disabled people were the key target. Cutting disability benefits by tens of billions of pounds was said to be a necessity – a prudent 'tough choice' to get the deficit down and rebuild the economy. This was as much a moral case as an economic one: as so-called hardworking 'strivers' watched their wages shrink, 'scrounging' disabled people were said to be milking the system. The image of a disabled person in the new age of austerity was not that of a human being who deserved support but of a liar and leach, living on the taxpayer's expense.

Since becoming ill, Bessie has washed her clothes in a bucket. The fifty-one-year-old has agoraphobia, Asperger's and digestive problems and had worked in her late dad's general store since she was twelve. But as her conditions got worse, even part-time hours became impossible – 'I was crippled with agoraphobia and panic attacks' – and by 2011 she had had to give up work entirely. For the next two years, she lived off her savings and some money she'd inherited from her dad, and when the money ran out, she applied for disability benefits.

The benefits themselves sound like government jargon – the out-of-work sickness benefit, Employment and Support Allowance (ESA) or Disability Living Allowance (DLA) – but for Bessie, they meant falling into hardship. As her illnesses forced her to live off social security, the most basic costs – food, electricity, clothes from a charity shop – were out of reach. Walk round Bessie's two-bed flat in Nottingham and 'a life of Riley' is not the picture that comes to mind. There's no oven in her kitchen, or a microwave. No freezer either; as she began to scrape by on social security, she got rid of that to save money. When her washing machine broke, she couldn't afford to replace it – not even with a second-hand one. Instead, she'd wash her clothes by hand; trousers, jumpers, with the water squeezed out by a spinner.

For all the talk of a comfortable life on benefits, disabled people like Bessie were almost destined to fall into hardship: scraping by on low benefits, lucky to have enough for food and rent. The Living Wage Foundation calculated that the figure needed to cover the true cost of living was £9.00 per hour (£10.55 in London) in 2018–19,[9] with the rise put down to the increased cost of household goods, rents and transport. Yet a disabled person like Bessie who's too ill to work was receiving £102 a week on her classification of ESA – the equivalent of £2.55 an hour for a full-time worker.

Or, to put it another way, a sum so meagre that researchers at the Disability Benefits Consortium in 2015 found it was leaving a third of recipients struggling to afford to eat.[10] That very thing heralded as an easy answer to any disabled person's problems – the so-called bloated welfare state – was in fact already so threadbare that it was actively pushing them into financial crisis. And yet it was these people – the long-term sick and disabled counting every last penny – who in the name of 'economic savings' were picked out by politicians to lose the little they had.

I returned to see Bessie several times over the next five years as austerity measures were introduced after 2012. Because she lived alone in a social housing property with a second bedroom, from April 2013 the bedroom tax saw her lose twelve pounds housing benefit a week. As she tried to balance the bills, it meant that, for the first time in her life, Bessie was pushed into debt: by October 2013 she had six months of rent arrears, as well as for water, gas and electricity. To be able to eat and have some heating through the winter, Bessie had to sell jewellery she had inherited from her late parents: a couple of rings, a gold sovereign. 'It's awful. All gone. I sometimes wonder what they'd think. But you have to survive, don't you?'

Things got harder. Over the next few years, Bessie was struck again and again by cuts. In 2016, as government so-called welfare reforms set in, Bessie was summoned for multiple 'reassessments' of her disability benefits. In the space of a year, she lost it all: first her out-of-work sickness benefit, ESA, and then in the summer of 2017 she had her lifetime award of DLA – the benefit that paid for specialist food for her digestive condition – removed too. What it has brought to Bessie is a profound anxiety. This was exacerbated by the distressing assessments themselves: the assessor 'was just bombarding me and I couldn't think properly. She made me cry.'

Bessie has been doing her best to build her life since she fell ill. She is halfway through a law degree with the Open University and is trying to start a business doing bookkeeping from home a few hours a week; but each time she gets up, she's knocked down again. The worry got so much that in the autumn of 2017 she called a district mental health nurse. She had to go on anti-anxiety tablets and apply for counselling, but with squeezed NHS mental health services, she was on the waiting list for over four months before her first appointment. 'I can't cope any more.'

Coping is often the only choice. After both of her disability benefits were stopped, Bessie sold more things from her home. She got rid of her television, as the licence costs money. She had pre-payment meters fitted – four pounds a week – to ration her heat and light. Sometimes, when awake in the early hours of the morning, she'd listen as it clicked to eight pounds at 2 a.m.

With the state pulling away, charities helped with the smallest of luxuries: a new mattress ('mine had a big spring coming out,' she says); some carpet for the bare floor; and, at last, a washing machine. While waiting to appeal her benefit rejections at tribunals, she saved money for a television licence and with it the distraction. 'You have to have something, don't you?'

At times Bessie has to list which of her possessions to sell next in lieu of her disability benefits. It's reminiscent of a sort of violence and strips away even a semblance of security. Research by the New Policy Institute (NPI) in 2016 paints a stark picture of how far exactly this problem spreads, chronicling the proportion of disabled people who are classed as living in what it terms 'severe material deprivation'.[11]

The term 'deprived' conjures up a stark image – in essence, a human being having what they need withheld from them. To be classed as being in 'severe material deprivation', according to the NPI, someone has to be unable to afford at least four of the following nine items: rent/mortgage/utility bills, the cost of keeping their home adequately warm, unexpected expenses, eating meat or proteins regularly, a holiday, a television set, a washing machine, a car, a telephone.

Almost one in five of working-age disabled people now meet this criterion.[12] That's three times as many as non-disabled people. For a scandalous number of disabled people in Britain today, to be 'merely' poor would be an improvement on their current situation.

A groundbreaking study by Heriot-Watt University for the Joseph Rowntree Foundation in 2018 found that 1.5 million people in Britain are so far below the poverty line that they are officially destitute.[13] This means that their weekly income is not enough to buy even basic essentials (for a single adult, seventy pounds) – or, grimly, as the researchers put it, an income so low that they can't meet their core material needs 'for basic physiological functioning'. Other criteria for being classed as destitute include eating fewer than two meals a day for several days a month and sleeping rough for one or more nights a month. Strikingly, a vast chunk of those designated destitute are disabled: Heriot-Watt University found that almost 650,000 people with physical or mental health problems in the UK are experiencing destitution. The true number is likely to be even higher. The research covered only people who had accessed formal help from crisis services or their local authority.

The research was an update to a 2016 study that first began to pinpoint the number of people in the UK living in extreme poverty after the 'welfare' reforms kicked in.[14] Suzanne Fitzpatrick, housing and social policy professor at Heriot-Watt, describes it as the 'new destitution': citizens who would previously have managed to avoid absolute destitution with the help of the welfare safety net but who can now easily find themselves in a position where they can't afford the basic essentials.[15]

One of the most damaging myths around poverty has always been that it is somehow inevitable – the idea that while some people enjoy a life of fortune, there will always be others who cannot afford food. But the state of extreme poverty developing for disabled people in this country is not an accident, but rather a direct reflection of the system that's been created in recent years. The Heriot-Watt research found that the most common causes of destitution were unsustainable debt repayments to public authorities, such as council tax arrears, as council tax changes meant that thousands of the poorest families had to contribute to the payment for the first time. Other factors included high rents and benefit delays, when disabled people are left with no money in their bank account because of benefit backlogs at the DWP.

Notably, in its report on the first study, the *Guardian* stated that the Heriot-Watt team's review of recent poverty research found little mention of destitution before 2012 – just as austerity cuts began to come into effect.[16] It's no coincidence that the only exception prior to 2012 was in relation to asylum seekers: people with restricted entitlement to social security. Through the age of austerity, disabled people were experiencing the type of abandonment typically saved for a group legally excluded from it. Under the regime of 'all in together' and 'difficult decisions', politicians were ushering in a wave of austerity measures against the very people Britain's 'safety net' was said to protect.

Overall, the 2010 coalition set in motion £28 billion worth of cuts to disabled people's income,[17] including the introduction of the bedroom tax, cuts to council tax support, the roll-out of the out-of-work sickness benefit ESA, and the tightening of benefit sanction rules. Analysis by the House of Commons Library for Frank Field MP in 2018 found that spending on welfare benefits for the UK's poorest families will have shrunk by nearly a quarter after a decade of austerity, with some of the most striking cuts hitting disability benefits.[18] To its architects, these changes marked the most ambitious reform of the welfare state for more than sixty years. To its disabled targets, an all-out assault on their lives. As Susan and Bessie can testify, these were not cuts that came singularly, but were experienced as multiple changes at once. When, say, the bedroom tax came in, the odds were it would be hitting people already falling short on rent because they've lost their council tax support. In politics, they call it 'cumulative impact'; in human terms, it's like being struck over and over again.

Ministers have consistently refused to conduct a full analysis of the changes, instead releasing an evaluation of each policy in isolation. This was the case even after the War on Welfare (WOW) petition – organized by a group of disabled volunteers – gained a debate in the House of Parliament in 2014 to challenge the government. As Claudia Wood from the think tank Demos put it, failing to analyse the cumulative impact of multiple disability cuts at best gives an incomplete picture.[19] At worst, it provides the illusion that these are cuts that are being fairly and evenly spread.

In its place, Demos and disability charity Scope tracked the damage of the cuts on disabled people in 2013, modelling a series of cumulative impact assessments across fifteen disability benefit 'reforms'. It found that by 2017–18, 3.7 million disabled people would experience a reduction in income.[20] Hundreds of thousands of them would be subject to up to six cuts simultaneously, or, as the researchers put it, the changes would hit 'the same group of disabled people over and over again'.[21] In cash terms, that translates as a Parkinson's patient or paraplegic having their income cut by thousands of pounds a year. The Centre for Welfare Reform calculated that, by 2018,[22] disabled people would on average be losing over £4,400 per person per annum. For severely disabled people, that goes up to almost £9,000. For many, this loss is even greater: by 2018, around 200,000 will have lost between £15,000 and £18,000 in income through a combination of cuts.

Over the following years, this is set to further take its toll. While the implementation of the first wave of disability cuts is completed, latest measures – ushered in by a succession of Conservative-led governments – will roll out. As of 2017, new recipients of one category of ESA have seen the benefit shrink by almost a third – down to seventy-three pounds a week – with half a million people who are too disabled or sick to work set to lose over £1,500 a year each.[23] Universal

Credit – the all-in-one benefit system scheduled to be rolled out to eight million households by 2023 – is due to make 450,000 disabled people financially worse off,[24] with some losing as much as £4,000 a year from the changes. At the same time, wider austerity measures, from ongoing benefit freezes to the gutting of local council services – relied on heavily by disabled people – will add to the burden.

The EHRC calculate that by 2022, the combined tax, social security and public spending policies carried out since 2010 will put a particular burden on disabled people. Families with a disabled adult as well as a disabled child will shoulder annual cash losses of just over £6,500 as a result of tax and benefit changes (or about 14 per cent of their net income).[25] Grimly, the study found that households of people with the most serious disabilities actually stand to lose the most.

This is palpably the ultimate death knell of the welfare state. Since its inception in late 1940s post-war Britain, the welfare state has produced some great strides for disabled people. Under the increasing growth of the state, the late 1940s to the mid-1960s marked a fundamental shift from the squalor of the workhouses – in which the destitute disabled were abandoned – to the belief that disabled people's living standards were increasingly a responsibility of the government. This also marked progress in cultural understandings of disability, as disabled people – throughout history said to be cursed, insane or simply lazy – began to be seen, at least in part, as members of society. The return of disabled servicemen motivated the first major state protection for disabled people; the 1944 Disability Employment Act promised sheltered employment and employment quotas for disabled people, while the National Insurance Act (1945) provided unemployment and sick pay for the long-term disabled.

Yet by the 1990s, while race and sex discrimination had long become illegal, disabled people in Britain were still the only group not to have basic rights enshrined in law. There was still no guaranteed access to work, transport or education.

Gains that did occur during this period were not handed down by a benevolent government but were the result of long-term lobbying and grass-roots activists. As I was at school in the summer of 1992, disabled activists with wheel-chairs and placards filled the streets, descended en masse to the television headquarters of Telethon '92 – ITV's then annual twenty-eight-hour fundraiser. The protesters were not simply challenging what they saw to be the programme's damaging depiction of disabled people – pitiable and tragic – but a country that, however well intentioned, was willing to grant charity handouts to disabled people, but not equality.

Regular protests followed: from wheelchair users kettled by police outside Westminster, to disabled people handcuff-ing themselves to buses. By the mid-1990s, disabled campaigners had successfully pushed for the Disability Discrimination Act – for the first time in Britain the law provided disabled citizens with access to the workplace, and with it a wage (employers were required to make 'reasonable adjustments' to work and premises). It also saw the launch of the landmark benefit Disability Living Allowance, a benefit introduced to help disabled people pay for the extra costs of mobility and care needs (from taxis to hospital appointments) that had previously pushed us into poverty. It embodied the principle of a universal safety net: no matter how rich or poor, in work or out, every disabled person was eligible to apply for help from the state.

It was fitting, then, that in a period that launched an unprecedented assault on disabled people's living standards, one of the first major policies of the austerity era was the abolition of DLA. In April 2013, the coalition government began the roll-out of a replacement benefit, Personal Independence Payment (PIP) – in practice launching the mass, mandatory retesting of around 3 million disabled people. The premise was simple: rather than a crucial safety net for millions of disabled citizens, this flagship benefit was being widely and brazenly exploited by swathes of scroungers.

At a time in which *Benefit Street*–style documentaries filled television screens and 'benefit fraudsters' emblazoned tabloid front pages, tellingly, the introduction of PIP came with the promise of tougher 'points-based' criteria and an end to the so-called 'soft touch' of DLA. As then work and pensions secretary Iain Duncan Smith, put it to the *Telegraph* in 2012, losing a limb should not automatically entitle people 'to a payout'.[26] That DLA was actually one of the most effectively targeted benefits with an estimated fraud rate of just 0.5 per cent was somehow irrelevant.[27]

Barely a year into its introduction, Parliament's public spending watchdog was calling the government's handling of PIP 'nothing short of a fiasco',[28] with reports of year-long delays and faulty rejections leaving family carers so poor they risked eviction from rent arrears and cancer patients unable to afford a taxi to hospital. In 2018, the Work and Pensions

Select Committee released a report chronicling what it called the 'untenable human costs' of the system, highlighting assessments plagued by basic errors, disrespect and ignorance of health problems.[29]

One submission made to the committee spoke of how a person with Down syndrome was asked by an assessor how they 'caught' it. Others with frequent suicidal thoughts described being quizzed over why they hadn't yet killed themselves. Another disabled woman recalled how her assessor reported that she walked a dog daily, when she can barely walk and does not own a dog. The consequence is the widespread removal of disability support: official government figures show that by December 2017 nearly half of disabled people put through these reassessments ended up having their support either cut or stopped entirely.[30]

This is not a horrible accident, but rather the architects' intention. Before testing for PIP began, ministers estimated that 500,000 fewer sick and disabled working-age people would receive benefits due to the abolition of DLA[31] – about a fifth of the total number receiving the benefit. It was 'welfare' reform carved out of a mounting suspicion of disabled people: after all, only if large numbers of disabled people were falsely claiming benefits could a government promise to reduce payments before anyone had even been reassessed.

That poverty is an individual moral failing has been relentlessly argued by those in power for nearly forty years. In this view the working class's personal characteristics say, a lack of ambition or effort – rather than an unequal society rigged in favour of the privileged is the root of inequality. It is a narrative that, by extension, neatly permits the state to wash its hands of a duty to assist those struggling under disadvantage.

Thatcher's infamous 'no such thing as society' remark in 1987 was preceded by a line that is a summation of this individualism: 'I think we've been through a period where too many people have been given to understand that if they have a problem, it's the government's job to cope with it.' Over twenty-five years later, as austerity measures got under way, this language began to sharpen in the twenty-first century. When then work and pensions secretary Iain Duncan Smith announced stricter conditions for unemployed jobseekers in 2013, he did it with the promise that it was an end to a 'something-for-nothing culture'.[32]

Even as anti-welfare attitudes festered over decades, disabled people have been traditionally exempt from such criticisms of 'dependency'. While, say, the figure of the working-class jobseeker or single mother was said to 'deserve' contempt, disabled people – culturally seen as pitiable and passive – were widely viewed as the 'good' recipients of state help. This hierarchy of desert is, of course, unhelpful and ultimately unsustainable: not only does it suggest that non-disabled people in poverty are deserving of any misery they endure; it also relies on disabled people conforming to certain prejudices – that we are needy, weak, grateful – in order to be exempt. Damningly, as the post-2010 austerity era kicked in, even this faulty division didn't last. Disabled people and their social security not only became fair game in the vilification of benefit claimants – they became the prime target. Newspapers and television shows hunted examples of the disabled 'milking the state'. Politicians talked openly of the 'bloated disability benefits bill'.

Against a backdrop of disenfranchisement, squeezed wages and a growing anti-'welfare' culture, Britain witnessed the emergence of 'the underserving sick': where not only is social and economic disadvantage a sign of personal failure, but also being disabled or ill. It was a double hit of individualism: not only could the fact that a person needed social security to stay afloat be blamed on their apparent lack of effort, but, as such, it also legitimized the belief that it's a cost that the state shouldn't have to pay. In this climate, disabled people were not equal human beings – or even pitiable and needy – but an underclass, lazy and deceitful. It combined a class hatred and revulsion of disability to uniquely scapegoat the disabled poor.

It was scapegoating that came with consequences. Two years into the coalition government in 2012, a group of disability charities reported a surge in hate crimes against disabled people, with public resentment over supposed mass abuse of the disability benefits system and negative media and government rhetoric said to be a key factor.[33] Charities including Scope, Mencap and the Royal National Institute of Blind People (RNIB) reported that they were now regularly contacted by people who had been taunted on the street about supposedly faking their disability, with others saying the climate is so hostile they avoid going out. 'When we go out, we get dirty looks in our wheelchairs. They're thinking, "You can stand. You're playing the system",' Susan tells me, years later. 'It's not just the media saying it. It's people in the street.'

The clever thing about lighting a culture of suspicion is that the state can simultaneously cut support for a marginalized group while claiming it's helping those who are 'truly' in need. From 2010 onwards, Conservative-led governments repeatedly argued that even while disability benefits were being cut, the 'truly disabled' would be protected. This was deceptive on two levels. It falsely suggested that the most severely disabled people would keep their social security. And it created the mythical idea that not every disabled person currently gaining support actually needed it. This policy created a hierarchy of disabled people: it was no longer enough to simply be disabled, you had to prove you were 'disabled enough'.

As I began to meet disabled people impacted by the cuts from 2012, I noticed that more and more disabled people I spoke to wanted to reassure me that they understood that the welfare bill was out of control but that they needed their benefits – that they knew others were faking but that people like *them* deserved help. It isn't hard to see why. As the first row of cuts began, the then disability minister Esther McVey bragged to the *Mail on Sunday* in 2013 that she was going after the 'bogus' disabled.[34] Four years later, Theresa May's then policy chief George Freeman was telling BBC 5 Live that disability benefits should go to the 'really disabled'.[35]

While disadvantage is held up as a moral failing, in reality its structural causes are never more blatant than with disabled people's poverty. As Susan and Bessie have found, the barriers to a decent income are frequent and brutal: be it a deficit in an adequate safety net of social security, being too ill to work, or a labour market that discriminates and excludes workers who need adaptations to enable them to earn a wage. But when it comes to a disabled person staying afloat, the issue isn't simply how little goes in but how much has to go out.

The existence of the 'poverty premium' is now well established: that in fact it actually costs more to be poor. For example, having to pay a higher tariff on a pre-pay heating meter instead of a cheaper direct debit. Much less is said about the 'disability poverty premium' – the reality that, while being more likely to be on a low income, on a day-to-day basis, disabled people are faced with extortionate outgoings. Research by Scope in 2018 found that life costs on average £570 more a month in Britain if you're disabled:[36] anything from buying specialist food to paying for taxis because public transport isn't accessible. For one in five, it's over £1,000 extra per month. In a climate in which disabled people's income has been gutted, it means that the most basic human needs, like being warm and dry, are widely becoming too expensive to meet.

Take something as vital as heating. When someone like Susan has to get out of her wheelchair and huddle up in bed with her dog just to keep warm, she is in many ways living in a catch-22. She needs the heating more because she's disabled – Scope has worked out that some disabled households spend more than twice as much on energy each year than the average family[37] – but in a society that is overseeing a new era of disability poverty, her disability means that her income is so low that she's less able to afford it.

When there isn't enough money coming in for a human being to live on, there tend to be two options: going without what you need – Susan's heating and food, Bessie's oven and furniture – or borrowing to pay for it. In recent years, debt has ballooned in the UK with 8.3 million families in 2017 living with problem debt,[38] fuelled by anything from low wages, the increase in the gig economy's erratic incomes, to council tax charges. It shouldn't be a surprise that what has hit the general population has hit those with disabilities and illness harder still: disabled people are twice as likely than non-disabled people to have unsecured debt totalling more than half of their household income, according to a Scope survey in 2013.[39]

This is not only a case of not having a cushion to cope with a sudden financial crisis – say a broken boiler or being made redundant – but of having an income so low that, week in week out, it won't even cover essential bills. It's a climate of borrowing money to survive: Scope finds that half of disabled people use credit cards or loans to pay for every-day items like food and clothes.[40] As Susan in London puts it to me, 'We're not talking about getting a loan for a three-piece suite. New curtains. This is the bare necessities.'

For Susan, it was a broken washing machine and freezer. The freezer is her lifeline – it stores her digestive medication and she can't eat safely without it – and the washing machine – there to regularly clean her clothes and sheets with her incontinence – is a bit of dignity. When both broke a few years back as the bedroom tax and care costs first hit, she could barely scrape together a spare fiver let alone a few hundred pounds. Instead, she turned to a doorstep loan company. In 2014, she took out two loans totalling £900. Five years later, the racked up interest rates means she's still paying it off: weekly instalments at eighty pounds. The company wanted bigger instalments, she says, but her carer helped talked them down. 'I couldn't pay [them] more because of all the benefit cuts.'

This is the double-edged sword of disability debt: while being more likely to face financial crisis, disabled people are shut out of ways to escape it. Disabled people are less likely to even have a current account than the non-disabled; without a stable income, 'good credit' is a phantom. As Susan puts it to me, 'Bank loans aren't for people like us.' Instead, people like Susan are routinely forced to turn to high-risk credit: one in ten disabled people have used doorstep loans, according to Scope research – that's three times as many as the general population.[41] In 2018, research by Citizens Advice into payday loans found that nearly half (48 per cent) of people struggling with 'home loan debt' have a long-term health condition or disability.[42]

By the time Susan manages to pay the loan back, the interest will have totalled £1,080 – more than the original loan itself. It'll take another year to pay off the debt but Susan is desperate for another loan. She's recently had to start using a specialist medical bed – the sides stop her from falling out at night – but she can't use it because she can't afford the linen to fit it. She knows that a new loan would cost her – the last doorstep leaflet that fell through her letterbox had an interest rate of 1,394 per cent – but she doesn't have a choice. 'You go round in circles,' she explains. 'Should I get another loan out? Once you get on that roundabout, you can't get off it.'

It isn't without its poignancy that if Susan had needed help only a few years earlier, she could have turned to the state. The 'social fund' – a £300-million-a-year nationally administered service of low-cost loans and grants paid through the JobCentre – used to provide an alternative to high-cost, high-risk credit. If social security is the 'safety net', the social fund

was the mattress positioned beneath it: a last-ditch support
for the poorest citizens in financial emergencies – for example, a fifty-pound loan to pay for transport for a hospital
appointment or £400 for a new boiler when the old one
packed in. This was tried-and-tested success for vast numbers
of families: more than 2.1 million crisis loans and 216,000
care grants were paid out in 2011–12.[43] For people living
with disabilities or illness, it was especially vital: one-third of
all claimants using the social fund were disabled.[44]

But as part of the 'welfare reforms' of 2013, the coalition
government abolished community care grants and crisis
loans. In its place, it devolved the responsibility to local
councils: a patchwork of 152 devolved programmes in
England that local authorities – already stretching to cover
core services in the face of spending cuts – had no obligation
to fund. At the same time, the government reduced funding
for the service by £120 million annually. That this happened
to come at a time of vast cuts to social security for disabled
people is perhaps austerity at its cruellest: as the government
brought in policies that pushed disabled people into crisis, it
simultaneously pulled the emergency funds that could help
them.

When Bessie in Nottingham had both of her disability
benefits removed in 2017, her only income was pulled overnight. Bumped off out-of-work sickness support, she became
eligible for the standard lower unemployment benefit,
Jobseeker's Allowance (JSA), but – with her disability benefits already stopped – she was told her JSA would take weeks
to come through. This is standard practice now: as disabled
people have their benefits removed, the system leaves them
with literally nothing to live on.

To survive, Bessie applied to the JobCentre for one ninety-three-pound hardship loan – to be knocked off at fifteen pounds a week from her benefit for the privilege – but that ran out fast. With another week to wait for her JSA and with no money for food or gas, Bessie phoned everyone she could think of for help – the JobCentre, the council, her GP – but with the social fund closed, she was told 'no one does crisis loans any more'. 'You get passed between different people, getting desperate,' she says. She'd heard from friends in other areas that councils provide hardship payments for gas and electricity in emergencies, but after ringing hers she was told that hers does not. If she lived only a couple of miles away from the borough she would cross into the city council that still does hardship payments.

It amounts to what's little more than a 'postcode lottery' on need, with the transfer to local welfare provision simultaneously cutting funding and making a disabled person's chance of surviving a crisis dependent simply on where they happen to live. By 2018, five years after the social fund closed and the service was devolved to local authorities, poverty campaigners declared local welfare schemes to be 'on the verge of collapse', with a quarter of English councils having reduced spending by 85 per cent or more since 2013, and nearly a further quarter closing their schemes entirely, according to research by Church Action on Poverty.[45]

Go to Bessie in Nottinghamshire or Exeter or Oxfordshire, for example, and there's now no scheme at all. A minority – like Islington and Trafford and Rutland – in contrast, have ring-fenced funding, even topping up national government cash when necessary. In Scotland, the Scottish Welfare Fund replaced the social fund, enabling councils to continue to award loans and grants of almost £40 million. Huge budget pressures faced by councils mean even authorities that have protected local welfare in the past will soon embark on drastic cuts; West Sussex County Council, for example, embarked on plans for an 80 per cent reduction in its £800,000 crisis fund from 2019.[46] Meanwhile, many English councils are so depleted they're now simply transferring the remaining scraps of their budget to local food banks or credit unions. Others are merely redirecting desperate families to local poverty and disability charities; a leaflet in the place of cash. In one case, Isle of Wight council offered a sixty-two-year-old homeless woman a voucher to buy a tent.[47]

It's no coincidence that as benefits were cut and emergency funds abolished, food banks are being relied on by the disabled and sick and their families. In the single biggest nationwide study on food banks to date, the University of Oxford in partnership with the Trussell Trust found in 2017 that the majority of people going to food banks are hit by disability or illness.[48] A whole century or so after the workhouses and 'cripples' were forced to go 'cap in hand' to survive, over half of households referred for emergency food parcels in Britain include a disabled person. Some 75 per cent are experiencing ill health.[49] I asked a manager of a London food bank if many disabled people came through the doors. 'We've had people who've had strokes, lots and lots of people with a mental health problem, several people being treated for cancer,' she told me. 'The worst case was a young homeless woman who had had both hands amputated and burns on her face and torso.' In recent months, she tells me, volunteers have delivered food parcels to disabled people's homes – they're starving but they haven't got the help to physically get to a food bank.

For different reasons, even a food bank is shut off from Bessie. Her mental health problems mean she can't eat solid foods – she has a fear of being sick – and she lives off specialist protein and nutrition drinks. Besides, even if a food bank gave her soup as a last resort, there's no cooker or microwave in the house to heat it. I speak to Bessie after she's gone two days without a single meal. With her benefit appeal coming up, she's saving her last few pounds to afford the medical certificate and postage she needs to send to the tribunal panel.

She's just called the GP to see if she can get her specialist food on prescription – 'even if they could give me half a week's worth' – but they refused; budget cuts mean they could only give it to someone if their weight had already fallen below a certain level, not as a way to prevent malnutrition. 'I suppose that's some good news. That I'm still a healthy weight,' she says. Her utility company has let her have a pre-paid card for gas but not electricity, so she's started to ration the light. In the end, with her benefits stopped and no crisis help available, a friend bought Bessie some packets of food. When that runs out, she tells me she'll drink loads of tea and water to stave off any hunger pangs. 'Basically people have to freeze and starve these days,' she says. 'There's nothing to fall back on any more, is there? It's all been taken away.'

Chapter 2

Work

The coroner said that when David Clapson died he had no food in his stomach. David, a former lance corporal in the Royal Signals, had worked in telecommunications for two decades and had left his last job to care for his elderly mum. When she died, David applied for Jobseeker's Allowance (JSA) to get by but after missing two meetings at the JobCentre, he had his benefits sanctioned for a month. David was a diabetic and without the £71.70 a week from his JSA he could not afford to buy food or to put credit on his electricity card to keep the fridge for his insulin working. Within three weeks, David had died from diabetic ketoacidosis, caused by a severe lack of insulin.

That was 2013, barely eighteen months after the coalition government had launched its first round of disability benefit cuts, and with it the shift in how Britain saw not only disability but disabled people on unemployment benefits. I covered David's death for the *Guardian*, one of the few media organizations to report on the story during a period in which the public gaze was being steered towards *Benefits Street*–style programmes and 'shop-the-benefit-fraudster' headlines. When I first looked into David's case a month after he died, I purposely resisted calling his death a tragedy.[1]

'Tragedy' suggests a one-off incident, a rarity that could not be prevented. What was done to David – and it was done, not something that simply happened – is a particularly horrific example of what has, almost silently, turned into a widespread crisis in Britain's response to disabled people struggling to work. The words of David's sister, Gail Thompson, at the time of his death summed up how brutal this climate was becoming. 'He died with six tea bags, an out-of-date tin of sardines and a can of tomato soup,' she had noted. 'There was a pile of CVs next to his body.'[2]

By 2018, five years after David's death, history was repeating itself. Diabetic Amy Driver, who had hearing and sight loss and severe fatigue, had her benefits sanctioned for four weeks after missing a meeting at the JobCentre to go to a hospital appointment. With no money for regular meals, Driver fell into a diabetic coma and died. She was twenty-seven.[3]

Britain is a country profoundly uncomfortable with disability and difference. This appears rarely more strongly than in the workplace and the unemployment system, in which disabled people are caught between two entirely contradictory stereotypes. On the one hand, we are pitiable and infirm, incapable of holding positions of influence or of making a capitalist contribution. On the other, we are lazy and wilful scroungers, leaching off the hard-working non-disabled public. This heightened noticeably as austerity measures began to roll out with a particular focus on out-of-work sickness and unemployment benefits. It was as if disabled people were simultaneously pitied for their infirmity and vilified as a useless burden; judged as incapable of basic tasks by non-disabled people and criticized for not being in employment.

In 2013, as the 'welfare' reforms were first rolling out, the *Daily Mail* ran an article with one GP, Dr Phil Peverely, said to be incensed by 'the thousands of patients "hell-bent" on trying to prove they are ill just to claim benefits.'[4] He told the paper that he was considering displaying a poster of the now late Stephen Hawking with the caption: 'This bloke is not on the sick.' The idea was a simple act of shame: if Hawking did not let his disability prevent him from becoming a world-renowned physicist, other disabled people had no such excuse.

The thinking was clearly preposterous. Each disability is different and factors such as wealth and education set Hawking's experience apart from most. But this example characterized a growing attitude of judgement and suspicion that began to fester after 2010, and one that rooted itself in the heart of government policy. Against a backdrop of austerity and a growing low-wage and insecure-contract economy, disabled people fell foul of an increasingly pernicious 'work and benefits' system: one that, rather than providing a 'safety net' for those too disabled to work and support for those who can, gladly abandoned them – the so-called 'skivers' – to the labour market at any cost. Heightened by austerity and given a sense of permission by government rhetoric, the narrative long built into capitalist societies was being squared sharply at disabled people: each of us are only valuable because of our contribution to the economy and those whose bodies cannot fit into this traditional mould must be judged or forced to comply.

The acceleration of the benefit sanctions that ended David's life is perhaps the most poignant symbol of this. Sanctions – by which the Department for Work and Pensions (DWP), through local JobCentres, removes a claimant's benefits for apparent behavioural infractions – have been a small part of the unemployment benefit system since the 1990s. At that time, the incoming Labour government adopted a 'work-first' strategy, monitoring claimants' job search activity, backed up by the removal of benefits. This was in many ways the beginning of a fundamental shift in the principle of the welfare state, suggesting that social security was not an entitlement but something that could be awarded or withheld based on a person's behaviour. In December 2012, the coalition government brought in a series of 'tougher' measures that vastly increased the scale and scope of sanctions. This made it easier to take more money from people on benefits, and to take it for longer.

Targeting specific previously protected groups – such as lone parents and disabled people – was a key part of the so-called 'reforms'. As wider disability benefit cuts began to bite, disabled people were now fair game to have their support docked like any healthy jobseeker. One of the government's flagship sanction measures was significantly increasing the amount of money they were able to take from sanctioned disabled and chronically ill people. For the first time, it became legal in Britain for the government to immediately remove 100 per cent of a disabled person's out-of-work benefits, Employment Support Allowance (ESA).

For an insight into how callous this is, ESA claimants are disabled people, who by the government's own definition are so disabled or ill they have no chance of earning an income themselves. (The only group excluded from sanctions were those disabled people judged incapable of any work preparation at all.) At the same time, people like David Clapson – claimants with long-term illnesses or disability but who have been placed on JSA – were victim to the same ratcheted-up punishment as any healthy jobseeker. Under the coalition, the minimum sanction length increased from one week to four, while in the most severe cases they could have their benefits removed entirely for three years.

The changes resulted in a rapid increase in the number of disabled people having their benefits suspended. Between 2013 and 2014, sanctions against disabled and chronically ill people rose by 580 per cent.[5] Benefits were now being withdrawn for a tiny infraction, most often when disabled people are deemed to fail to take part in what the DWP terms 'work-related activity': anything from skills training or drawing up a CV to participating in community work placements.

Since 2010, disabled people in Britain have been hit with more than one million sanctions, according to research by the Demos think tank and academic Ben Baumberg Geiger.[6] Separate figures by the Department for Work and Pensions in 2017 showed that almost 6,000 people on the out-of-work sickness benefit, ESA, have had their benefit stopped for at least six months (between December 2012 and December 2016).[7] Destitution is the inevitable and proven result of docking benefits. In 2018, a five-year study led by the University of York, the UK's largest ever research into the effects of conditionality, found that sanctions were likely to reduce those affected to poverty, ill health or, for the particularly vulnerable, even the grimly dubbed 'survival crime'.[8]

Among its recommendations, the York study called for an immediate moratorium on benefit sanctions for disabled people, who, it noted, are disproportionately affected by the policy: the 2018 Demos research found that unemployed disabled people are up to 53 per cent more likely to be docked money than claimants who are not disabled.[9] There's countless evidence of just what this looks like in practice. A cross-party Parliamentary inquiry into benefit sanctions undertaken in 2015 heard from a twenty-three-year-old pregnant woman who was receiving ESA for mental health problems following the stillbirth of her first baby eight months earlier.[10] She was sanctioned after missing one 'work-focused interview' because on that day she had found it too difficult to leave her flat. With no money to feed herself or her unborn child or even for a bus fare, she ended up walking two miles to a food bank for an emergency food parcel.

By 2018, as the sanctions regime continued and MPs undertook another inquiry, a man with epilepsy told the committee how he had been sanctioned after missing a work-related meeting because he was in hospital, due to multiple seizures. Another disabled woman recounted how she had been forced to spend nearly a year without benefits after being wrongly sanctioned. With no money to pay rent in her temporary accommodation, she became homeless and was forced to sleep in her college library. On other nights, she rode the night bus just to have somewhere to sleep. She was recovering from an accident and on heavy-duty morphine but was given no special allowances to keep her social security. As she told MPs, 'If you ask them [the DWP] for help they will say, "No, we will punish you instead." '[11]

This sense of 'punishment' has been an underlying force in the shift to increased 'conditionality' in the 'welfare' system in recent years. As then disability minister Esther McVey put it in 2013 when defending sanctions, 'What does a teacher do in a school? A teacher would tell you off, or give you lines and detentions, or whatever it is, but at the same time they have your best interest at heart.'[12] Here, disabled people are not human beings who need support to find a job, or compassion during times they are too unwell to work, but naughty children-cum-scrounger who need discipline as motivation to get off the 'easy life' of benefits.

An unemployment system based on the premise of pulling social security from people who don't show 'correct behaviour' is damaging enough for a standard jobseeker. But for disabled claimants, it's little more than a punishment for being disabled: their disability means they physically or mentally often have no way to comply with the conditions they have to meet to avoid being sanctioned. When the state deems it a success to stop the money a disabled person needs to eat, it hasn't only abandoned its duty of care but morphed into an agent actively causing harm. This is government of the grotesque.

The roll-out of Universal Credit (UC) – the 'all-in-one' social security system that will impact millions of out-of-work and low-earning disabled people[13] – is set to embrace a particularly pernicious sanctioning culture. Between 2015 and 2017, more than 100,000 UC claimants have already had their benefits stopped.[14] That this is set to continue becomes even more disturbing when you consider that the system has been proven not to even work. Ministers have repeatedly claimed that sanctions are effective in 'focusing' people for work – as if going hungry clarifies a lazy mind – despite repeated evidence from the National Audit Office,[15] among others, that they do no such thing.

'Most men who have once gained the habit of work would rather work – in ways to which they are used – than be idle, and all men would rather be well than ill,' Sir William Beveridge wrote in the Beveridge report in 1942. Over seventy-five years on, Britain has actively regressed from these aspirations. The acceleration of the benefit sanction system is emblematic of a wider shift in this country towards a perception of disabled people as 'work-shy' scroungers – boiled down and packaged as major government policy. Research by the London School of Economics in 2016 found that half of Britons believed that out-of-work sickness benefit claims had risen in the past fifteen years.[16] In fact they have fallen.

It is not hard to see why people might fall for this misinformation. When ministers announced cutting part of the out-of-work sickness benefit, ESA, by a third to just seventy-three pounds a week in April 2017, it was on the premise that it would give disabled people an 'incentive' to get a job.[17] Such an assumption supposes that the reason someone with Parkinson's has been out of work for a year is not that they cannot hold a pen because of their tremors, but because they're too idle to get off benefits. At the same time, the government substantially stepped up its scrutiny of disabled people receiving out-of-work benefits, resorting to using supermarket CCTV, gym memberships, airport footage and surveillance video from public buildings, as well as posts from personal social media accounts, to suggest people are lying about their disabilities. The number of benefit investigators increased by over 40 per cent (from 2,600 to 3,700) between 2015 and 2016; notably more than five times as many officials than were deployed to investigate fraud by the super-rich, despite the fact that benefit fraud costs the government around £1.3 billion a year compared to around £34 billion for tax evasion.[18]

It has become normal for politicians to use inflammatory language about people on sickness benefits, or for newspaper editors to dedicate front pages to warning of the burden of the masses of faking disabled people supposedly milking the welfare budget. By 2015, then welfare secretary Iain Duncan Smith was imploring business owners to get disabled employees 'signed off sick' back to work – in his words, so they could no longer 'wallow in a life on benefits'.[19] The *Daily Express*, meanwhile, devoted an editorial to welcome the 'crackdown on sick-note culture'.[20] The phantom work-shy – long a target of those keen to shrink Britain's safety net – now included people too sick to make it to work in the morning.

There is perhaps no starker signal of this than the post-2010 rise of the Work Capability Assessment – or 'fit-for-work' test – used to determine whether disabled people are eligible for out-of-work sickness benefits or must look for a job. The concept of the state providing a safety net for disabled citizens unable to earn a wage has been building in Britain for the last hundred years. While the turn of the twentieth century saw the first sickness benefits introduced as part of the radical National Insurance Act, it wasn't until the 1970s that social security specifically for unemployed disabled people started, with Edward Heath's government

bringing in the formative Invalidity Benefit for citizens too
disabled to work. It was the benchmark of a civilized welfare
state in which, along with the pillars of the NHS, citizens
collectively paid in to have the security of a safety net in
times of ill health.

By the mid-1990s, John Major's Conservatives were
ushering in the new Incapacity Benefit (IB) and with it a
fundamental change: for the first time officials could ask for
claimants' disabilities to be 'confirmed' using a special testing procedure dubbed the All Work Test. Almost twenty
years on, this shift to the state monitoring disabled benefits
claimants grew, with New Labour introducing the Work
Capability Assessment (WCA) – a new digitalized, 'tick-box'
assessment – to decide who was eligible for its new incapacity benefit, ESA.

But it was the post-2010 coalition government who
orchestrated an unprecedented acceleration of this testing
regime. While Tony Blair's government sought to introduce
ESA for new claims only, within its first year in office the
coalition – promising to remove £3.5 billion from the benefits bill by 2014–15[21] – chose to push the almost two and a
half million existing Incapacity Benefit recipients through
the new system. The roll-out of the Work Capability
Assessment was the embodiment of the post-crash narrative
that disabled people were suspects. On the back of a bid to
drive down the so-called 'bloated welfare bill', every single
disabled person on out-of-work sickness benefits in the
country was told they were to be tested to see if they were in
fact 'fit for work'.

Ask Christina what the reality of a 'fit-for-work test' is and
the answer comes without pause: 'It's Russian roulette with

our lives.' The fifty-five-year-old was in the middle of training for a new job in a hotel in Northampton when she fell suddenly ill in 2017 with a pulsating pain in her gut. Within a month, she'd been diagnosed with gall bladder disease as well as inflammation of the stomach.

Christina was already living with debilitating health problems before this latest hit. Fibromyalgia leaves her with 'unbearable pain' through her spine, neck and joints. Her ankles are visibly swollen. It's a 'brain fog' too, she explains: where she knows the words she wants to say but they get lost somewhere between her brain and mouth. Some days, she says, she's sitting upright and will simply fall asleep. 'The body aches tip to toe as if I've been beaten up or thrown from a horse. I genuinely feel about ninety years old.' Nevertheless, when the government decided to test Christina's capability for work they did not liaise with her consultants at hospital. Instead she was invited to an assessment centre run by a private company.

From its beginning, the roll-out of the WCA has been delivered through a large-scale outsourcing programme, with the government hiring multi-billion-pound firms such as Atos and later Maximus to deliver the computer-programled assessments. This is tick-box, brown-envelope bureaucracy at its worst. A disabled person's fate is decided by questions of whether they can, for example, lift an empty box. Rather than being overseen by a doctor or specialist, the whole thing is typically conducted by a nurse, paramedic or 'medical professional'. In Christina's case, the tester did not even understand what fibromyalgia was.

Read through the report made by the assessor and the mistakes are copious. At one point, it states that Christina can walk 200 metres easily without difficulty. 'I stood up once [in the assessment] . . . I wasn't even asked about walking difficulties,' she tells me. There's no mention of the fact that standing on her feet even to make dinner results in three to four hours of pain. Such omissions and errors are par for the course, however. In 2016, the National Audit Office (NAO) found that not one of the companies carrying out the tests met the government's own quality assessment threshold, with communications including errors, spelling mistakes, and unintelligible acronyms.[22] Only half of all the medical professionals hired to carry out the assessments had completed their training. The result is disabled people being incorrectly dumped off their benefits en masse: as the assessments rolled out, headlines spoke of terminal cancer patients and people in comas found 'fit for work'. The latest figures in 2018 show that, staggeringly, 70 per cent of disabled people declared 'fit to work' who appeal have the decision overturned at tribunal.

Within weeks of her WCA, Christina became another statistic. A 'decision maker' at the Department for Work and Pensions called her at home and told her she'd been judged 'fit for work'. The assessor had given her 'zero points'. Christina tells me she called the DWP to ask how this was possible. 'The woman said, "If Stephen Hawking can work, so can you."' It means that a severely ill woman is now being forced to look for jobs that she can't possibly do. 'I'm unfit for work according to my GP, yet the DWP can apparently disregard that,' she says.

Christina has the support of her son, Martin, as she waits for surgery on her gall bladder while having to navigate the JobCentre, and is as resilient as she can be. Some have been

less fortunate. Flick through local papers in recent years and
deaths of disabled people ghost through the pages. On 18
January 2017, the *Camden News Journal* reported that
Lawrence Bond – diagnosed with a heart condition, obesity
and shortness of breath – died six months after he'd been
assessed 'fit for work'.[23] The fifty-six-year-old had a fatal
heart attack on the way home from Kentish Town JobCentre
and was found dead in the street. In August that year fifty-
four-year-old David Metcalf ran into the sea after being
found 'fit for work'.[24] The *Hartlepool Mail* reported that
Metcalf had been on out out-of-work sickness benefits for
almost a decade due to anxiety, stress and panic attacks
before the new test saw the benefits stopped. Sandra Burns,
who had chronic back pain with five fused vertebrae, was
repeatedly tested and rejected for disability benefits, and
won on appeal each time, getting into debt during the
process.[25] *Luton Today* noted how the fifty-seven-year-old's
body was found by police at the foot of her stairs after a
suspected heart attack, surrounded by debt letters telling her
the gas, electricity, water, telephone and television were in
danger of being cut off.

For one person to die in this manner is obscene, but this
is more than a handful of cases. Death has become part of
Britain's benefits system, in which people who have life-
threatening illnesses can be deemed 'fit for work', while those
who need support for mental health problems are instead
thrown to the JobCentre with their benefits cut. Researchers
from the University of Liverpool in 2015 found that the new
'fit-for-work' tests could be linked to 590 extra suicides and
725,000 additional antidepressant prescriptions in
England.[26]

At the same time, coroners have repeatedly pointed to 'fit-for-work' tests as a contributory factor in a number of disabled people's deaths. For example, Tim Salter, who was blind, depressed and agoraphobic, had his benefits removed in 2013 after being deemed capable of work. Unable to pay the rent, the fifty-three-year-old took his own life before he was due to be evicted. As the South Staffordshire coroner investigating Salter's death said, 'A major factor in his death was that his benefits had been greatly reduced leaving him almost destitute.'[27]

Suicide is complex, and the Samaritans rightly discourage reports that put any such death down to a single cause, but it is not hard to predict what the impact might be on someone of losing their only income. Remove social security from a disabled person too disabled or ill to work and it's like pushing someone off a cliff and feigning surprise when they hit the beach. The assessments themselves are categorically proven to have made disabled people sicker. Research by charity Leonard Cheshire in 2015 found that almost three-quarters of those who had gone through the process said they found the assessment had a negative impact on their health.[28] More than six in ten said they had ended up with more pain afterwards. The idea of a safety net has gone so severely wrong: where people who need benefits because they're disabled are made more disabled simply trying to get help from the state.

Professor Jonathan Portes, formerly the chief economist at the DWP and later the director of the National Institute of Economic and Social Research, has described the reassessment programme as 'the biggest single social policy failure of the last fifteen years'.[29] In 2014, the chaos was such that Atos bought its way out of its £400 million contract early, with the company becoming so synonymous with disabled people forced into work that disability campaigners were picketing its offices holding placards reading 'Atos Kills'. A Facebook group named 'Atos Miracles' – ironically celebrating the apparent miraculous cure achieved by those assessed and found to be fit – garnered over 30,000 followers.

Fatefully, it was also discovered that the scheme was not even a money-saving initiative. By 2017, with a new private company, Maximus, having taken Atos's place, the NAO calculated that the government was actually spending more money assessing whether people are 'fit to work' than it is saving in reductions to the benefits bill.[30] While disabled people like Christina have their income cut, the government blew an estimated £1.6 billion of taxpayers' money on the faulty assessments between 2016 and 2019.

On top of this, by 2020 the government will have had to pay out £970 million in arrears to 180,000 disabled people it wrongfully withheld support from in the transfer to the new out-of-work sickness benefit – a bill that will go up to £1.7 billion by 2025 once the cost of paying them at the higher correct rate is factored in.[31] The scandal was a microcosm of the wider cruel and costly 'welfare reforms' forced onto disabled people in recent years. As the Conservatives brought in their new tougher 'fit-for-work' test, they did so without checking that claimants were receiving the right level of benefit, despite it being legally required. Although the error was picked up in 2013, a culture of indifference and incompetence meant it took another five years and an investigation by the NAO for ministers to admit the need to provide £5,000 in compensation to each person affected.[32] In the meantime, hundreds of thousands of the country's poorest disabled people needlessly lived in further hardship. Fifteen thousand people died while waiting.[33]

One of the great ironies of the austerity era was that while it attempted to force disabled people too unwell to work into a job, the disabled people whose conditions mean they *were* actually able to work were routinely shut out of employment. Unemployment among the disabled community is an epidemic: just under half of disabled people aged sixteen to sixty-four are in work, compared to over 80 per cent of non-disabled people, as of 2017 (that means fewer than five out of ten disabled people have a job compared with eight in ten non-disabled people).[34] Break this down by disability and for some it gets worse still: just 16 per cent of people with autism are in full-time paid work,[35] while less than 6 per cent of learning-disabled people are in full-time employment.[36]

This scale of unemployment isn't simply about not being hired; it's about shutting out disabled people from whole swathes of society. Engineering a system where disabled people are unlikely to find work means withholding their chance at economic independence or finding a place in the community and the social status given to paid work. Rather than the stability and higher living standards of a wage, they are pushed into surviving on low-rate benefits. It's disabled people's exclusion from the labour market that in many ways is fundamental to perpetuating a disabled underclass.

Britain has a long-standing history of inequality in employment for disabled people. As Sonali Shah and Mark Priestley write in their book *Disability and Social Change*,[37] the 1944 Disabled Person's Employment Act made gains by establishing a national register of 'substantially handicapped' persons, as well as a statutory 3 per cent quota for their employment. Based on the principle that 'disability is a handicap, not a barrier, to employment',[38] it designated certain occupations 'reserved' for disabled people and formalized sheltered work facilities for those deemed unable to gain work in the open market.

Against a backdrop of mass unemployment and declining industry, however, the 1970s and 1980s saw a substantial drop in the number of employers fulfilling their obligations under the national disability quota scheme. Meanwhile, a surge of disabled men transferred to out-of-work sickness benefits after losing their livelihoods to closing industries. There were gains in the late 1990s and early 2000s under New Labour – the employment rate for disabled people rose from 38 per cent to 47 per cent[39] – but it stalled once more under the coalition and Theresa May's government, despite a succession of Conservative administrations pushing to remove disabled people from out-of-work sickness benefits.

While ministers in recent years have repeatedly promised to halve the disability employment gap, the government quietly dropped this pledge in 2017. Instead, they promised to get an extra one million disabled people in work by 2027.[40] It's no wonder: the All-Party Parliamentary Group for Disability has calculated that if you take the rate the disability employment gap has fallen in recent years and assume the rate stays the same, it will be another forty years before the gap is even halved.[41]

As the image of the 'work-shy' disabled festers, in reality, unemployed disabled people relentlessly send out CVs and

receive rejections: Scope research in 2017 found that disabled people have to apply for 60 per cent more jobs than
non-disabled people before being hired.[42] This is little
surprise: in 2019, Leonard Cheshire found that nearly a
quarter of employers in Britain admit they'd be less likely to
hire a disabled person,[43] despite the law clearly stating that
people with disabilities should not be discriminated against
when seeking employment.

Forty-one years old, Christopher – who has autism and a
learning disability, as well as a speech impediment – has been
struggling to find work for the past twenty years. 'It drives
you round the wall. Year after year,' he says, wearily. 'You're
forced to worry about the future every day.'

Christopher speaks to me from his parents' house in
Cornwall. At his age, he wants to move out to a place of his
own ('I feel like a failure,' he tells me) but he knows he's stuck
until he's got a secure wage coming in. Since he left school in
the 1990s, he's struggled to keep hold of jobs. He finds it hard
to 'fit in' with colleagues when they don't understand autism,
while employers judge him as less capable once they hear his
stutter. Contract work is sporadic: a spell as a postman lasted
eight months and a bed raiser fitter only a month. For the last
year, he's worked as a cleaner at a plastic factory two miles
down the road: a contract for twelve hours a week at minimum wage. He earns £181 every fortnight – or just about
enough to keep his car running to look for other work.

The bureaucracy of the tax and benefit system means he's
shut off from state support: if he hits sixteen hours a week,
his employer has to start paying national insurance and he
becomes eligible for working tax credits: £400 every four
weeks. As it stands, he has to sign on at the JobCentre to

prove he's looking for work. In May 2017, they sent him for a four-week training course on the Work Programme – the government's flagship 'welfare-to-work' scheme – but it did nothing to help him secure a job. The programme was promoted as being designed specifically for disabled people but in practice Chris was put alongside people with vastly different conditions: from mental health problems to chronic illness. 'You just get lumbered in,' he says. 'I asked, what sort of help do have you for autism? They said, "Not much." '

This is set to get worse. The Work Programme and Work Choice – the programme specifically for disabled jobseekers – was abolished in autumn 2017 and replaced by the succinctly named Work and Health Programme. Like the Work Programme before it – famed for its 93 per cent failure rate for finding long-term jobs for claimants with disabilities[44] – the Work and Health Programme has been contracted out to private companies and has a reduced budget: cut from £750 million in 2013–14 to less than £130 million by 2017.[45] That translates as 45,000 fewer disabled people being allowed onto specialist employment provision each year between 2017 and 2020.[46] Meanwhile, there's no commitment by the government that, post-Brexit, the European Social Fund support – currently worth over £500 million a year in specialist support for disabled jobseekers[47] – will be replaced beyond 2020.

At the same time, annual cuts of £140 million a year over the next decade will see government JobCentres – the bricks and mortar of local unemployment support – across the country merge or shut their doors entirely,[48] forcing the long-term sick and disabled to trek further for basic support or even access the Internet or a computer. Tellingly, these

JobCentre cuts were launched just at the time ministers began to roll out a benefits system that more than ever required claimants to access the Internet; to receive Universal Credit, would-be claimants must apply online as well as use the website to apply for jobs, prepare CVs and register for required training courses – or risk a benefit sanction. However, 22 per cent of disabled adults in the UK had never used the Internet in 2017,[49] with the poorest households particularly unlikely to have access. It means that the people who most need Universal Credit are the most likely to be punished for not having the means to apply for it.

Put this against existing changes to on-the-job support for disabled workers and it's a vision of a widespread removal of employment support for disabled people in Britain. Access to Work – the government-funded scheme that from 1994 provided grants for practical support, from computer software to British sign language interpreters, for disabled people at work – has seen cuts by stealth since 2014, with Deaf workers in particular reporting reductions in the amount of support available, payment delays and fewer hours of help. While politicians fetishize pushing disabled people into the labour market, the support needed to make this possible is shredded.

Ask a government minister about disability employment rates and the claim is typically that almost 600,000 disabled people moved into work in the UK between 2013 and 2017.[50] But dig a bit further and much of this is marked by 'fluctuating employment': disabled people who may have a job now but soon enough risk losing it (disabled people are more than twice as likely to fall out of work than non-disabled people[51]). As of 2017, disabled people are dropping out of work faster than they're moving into it: Office for National Statistics (ONS) figures show that for every 100 disabled people moving into work, 114 leave.[52]

The figure of '600,000' also fails to say anything about the quality of jobs on offer – whether these are full-time contracted jobs that are equipping workers with a living wage and sick leave or, say, piecemeal labour forcing disabled people to live hand to mouth. For example, Christopher has not had a full-time job since 2009. Instead, he's been bouncing between part-time work for the past decade: A porter at a care agency. Car valet. Market worker. Selling clothes in Tesco's. A music apprentice. Since we first met in 2016, Christopher's emails me regularly as he searches for more part-time work to add to his hours at the factory. He applies for jobs relentlessly – anything going that he has a slight chance at – but gets knocked back each time. In September 2017, he emailed to tell me his first bit of luck: he's been offered work at a bakery. Fourteen hours a week sorting the pots in the dishwasher and taking the bread out of the ovens. The work would push him over his sixteen-hour target for in-work benefits but it was in South Brent, Devon. To get there, the daily journey included a half-hour car drive and then a ferry ride. What's more, the shifts would have to be slotted into his hours at the factory. Some days, Christopher would have to do three to five hours at the bakery in Devon, travel back to Cornwall, get to the factory and clean for three hours. Over the weekend, it would mean finishing at 10 p.m. one day and starting the next at 5 a.m. Christopher was already working out a plan how to wake up every morning: 'I'll get two alarms and set them fifteen minutes apart.'

Across the economy we have seen the rise of the

casualization of work in Britain, with the proliferation of
workers on zero-hours contracts, doing agency work or
earning the minimum wage on scattered hours. A study by
the University of Manchester in 2017 found that poor-quality jobs are actually worse for your health than unemployment, with a shift to jobs that are high-stress and low-pay
routinely damaging to workers' bodies and minds.[53] But
what makes an insecure job difficult for workers generally
can make it debilitating for someone with a disability or
health condition. Agency workers, for example, are not entitled to sick pay.

Christopher says the stress is a constant now and this way
of living is having an impact on his health. The factory is a
'sauna' and the noise from the machines is piercing despite
the use of ear protectors that block the vibrations as he
works. He recently pulled a muscle in his shoulder and,
suffering constant pain, he went to A & E to get a script for
higher pain meds but he couldn't afford the £8.50 prescription charge. Instead, he got some Ibuprofen from Morrison's
to get through his shifts: £1.50 a box. 'You're making these
decisions all the time,' he says. 'It's horrible.' I continue to
talk to Chris over the next year as he struggles to keep hold
of his cleaning job while constantly looking for more work.
One evening in autumn 2018, he had an accident at the
factory, this time burning himself with the cleaning bleach,
followed by another trip to A & E. 'It makes you feel even
more awful having to be on the minimum wage because you
feel you're bottom of the heap,' he says. 'Actually, it makes
you mad inside.'

Around a third of disabled people – 30 per cent of disabled men and 35 per cent of women – are paid below the

national living wage in Britain,[54] holding down jobs while chronically ill or disabled and being rewarded for it with poverty wages. It is still routine for disabled workers to be paid less than non-disabled colleagues. The EHRC August 2017 report on pay gaps found that the disability pay gap – the difference between what non-disabled and disabled workers earn – was at 13.6 per cent.[55] That inequality gets even worse if you're a disabled person who also happens to be a woman or from an ethnic minority background. Disabled men from the Bangladeshi community, for example, experience a pay gap of a staggering 56 per cent compared with non-disabled white men.[56]

Instead of challenging the disability pay gap, politicians often actively advocate it. The idea that it should be legal for employers to pay disabled people less than the minimum wage, for example, has been a recurring mainstream claim in recent years, particularly about people with learning disabilities. In 2014, a key Conservative 'welfare' minister, Lord Freud, was recorded as stating that some disabled people are 'not worth the full wage'.[57] They could, he suggested, be paid as little as two pounds an hour. In 2018, Chancellor Philip Hammond linked the low productivity of the economy with the increased number of disabled people in the workforce, much to the outrage of disability organizations.[58] This is nothing less than the promotion of a second-class wage system, justified by the false premise that disabled people are less productive than 'normal people' and employers need a financial incentive to take 'the risk' of hiring them.

The language is more disguised but this 'two-tier' wage system is also advocated by left-wing voices. The chair of the Work and Pensions Select Committee, Labour MP Frank

Field, published an essay in September 2017 recommending paying disabled people less than the minimum wage as a way of reducing disability unemployment.[59] You might almost respect the gall: not only are disabled people told to accept segregated wages but are told it is actually for our benefit. 'The people who are most disadvantaged by the national minimum wage are the most vulnerable in society,' as Conservative MP Philip Davies put it in 2011 as he called for employers to be allowed to pay workers with mental health problems less than other employees. 'My concern about it is it prevents those people from being given the opportunity to get the first rung on the employment ladder.'[60]

In reality, such measures are likely to only further segregate disabled people in the workplace, giving a free pass to exploitative employers while, at the same time, putting downward pressure on the wages of other workers. Speaking on a panel at the Conservative Party conference in 2018, former 'welfare' chief Iain Duncan Smith suggested that bosses should hire disabled workers because 'they often work longer hours' and 'forgo quite a lot of holiday because they love the whole idea of being in work'.[61] When it comes to the disability pay gap, there's an urgent need to address the causes. The EHRC found in 2017 that offering flexible hours to all job applicants will increase job opportunities for disabled people, as well as help tackle the gender pay gap.[62] As it stands, advertised flexible working hours are a rarity; while all employees currently have the right to request flexible working after twenty-six weeks of work, some employers don't offer flexible working – such as job shares or home working – for senior roles or at all.

Meanwhile, the building blocks that help people earn a decent wage are still disproportionately cut off from disabled people. Almost twice as many non-disabled people have a degree than disabled people (19 per cent versus 35 per cent),[63] while almost one in five disabled people have no qualification whatsoever[64] – a rate nearly three times higher than for people without disabilities. This contributes to young disabled people quickly being put on the scrapheap. Research from Leonard Cheshire in 2017 found that by the age of twenty-six, disabled people are nearly four times more likely to be unemployed than their non-disabled peers.[65] The same Leonard Cheshire study found that half of eighteen- to thirty-year-old adults said their teachers may have had 'lower expectations' of them because of their disability, while almost half also said that they weren't encouraged to go on a course or pursue their chosen career.

In Cornwall, Chris left school without any qualifications ('I think the best I got was a G in English'), and it's directly reduced his chance of getting work. He went back to college in his twenties to get his GCSEs: a D in English and C in Maths. 'It's a good job mum's alive or I'd be out on the street,' he says. 'But then it's been like that for twenty-five years.'

While disability unemployment is individualized – painted as a lack of effort from the 'work-shy' disabled – in reality, it's these structural barriers that keep disabled people out of the workplace. The inequality that disabled people face at work does not exist in a vacuum; it connects to the fact that in the twenty-first century, Britain is still built in a way that largely shuts us out.

The disability charity Papworth Trust reports that one of the most common barriers to work for disabled people is as mundane as a difficulty with transport;[66] the fact that, say, wheelchair users can't get on most of the London Underground, or a bus doesn't have a hearing loop. A government audit of 30,000 restaurants and shops in 2014 found what it called 'shocking' access to the high street, including a fifth of shops having no wheelchair access and only 15 per cent of restaurants and shops installing hearing loops; there's little chance of getting a job as a waiter or shop assistant if the premises aren't even accessible.[67]

At the same time, cash-strapped local authorities are cutting services that disabled people rely on to get them to work, from public transport to social care. In 2018, the Campaign for Better Transport found council funding for bus services had almost halved since 2010.[68]

The past twenty years have seen the introduction of landmark legislation to enshrine disabled people's basic employment rights in Britain – 1995's Disability Discrimination Act (DDA), followed by the 2010 Equality Act, made it illegal for the first time for employers to discriminate against a disabled person. Before then, in the so-called modern age of the mid-1990s, a prospective employer could refuse to hire someone because he was Deaf or sack a wheelchair user because they couldn't climb the stairs to the office, and the victim would have no protection under the law.

But while the law has offered some progress, disabled people in the workplace are still facing a decidedly hostile environment, be it being verbally abused, overlooked for promotion, or illegally pushed out of the job altogether. Research by GMB, the union representing neurodivergent workers, in 2017 found that 70 per cent of workers with conditions such as autism, attention deficit hyperactivity disorder (ADHD), dyslexia and dyspraxia report experiencing discrimination.[69] One in two disabled people have experienced bullying or harassment at work because of their disabilities, according to research by the charity Scope in 2017.[70] The same study found that this discrimination has reached such heights that over half of workers with a disability feel at risk of losing their job. The fragmenting of employment rights that's come with the boom in zero-hour contracts and agency work only exacerbates this insecurity, where disabled agency workers have no protection from unfair dismissal or redundancy.

Pearl has been sacked twice in nine months because she's disabled. The twenty-eight-year-old has dystonia – her hands, neck, shoulder, and right foot repeatedly spasm – and has worked in the media with high-profile companies since university. She needs adaptations at work such as dictation equipment as she can't type for long periods. She cannot walk for long stretches either. But for the last few years, as she's built her career, she's found that employers assume she's 'faking' her disability or is a 'nuisance' for mentioning it. 'People think I'm exaggerating, "oh, she's putting it on,"' she says. 'I've heard so many times from bosses, "just leave your [disability] at the office door."'

I first speak to Pearl in December 2016 from her parents' home in Cardiff as she's just been fired from a media group in London after enduring months of verbal abuse. At one point, she had a panic attack in the office and her dystonia – exacerbated by anxiety – made it difficult for her to type or concentrate. Instead of support, she was given a critical work review on the spot and told how 'slow' she could be. Her doctor prescribed Valium for the stress and she eventually had a breakdown. As the anxiety exacerbates her disability, her muscles deteriorated to the extent she had to move back in with her parents.

Barely nine months later, it happened again. Pearl had moved back to London in September 2017 for a new job – a three-month contract as a marketing assistant for a charity – but within a week of starting work, despite knowing about her disability, her bosses gave her tasks including lugging heavy equipment, walking two miles and standing all day. It escalated on an 'away day' in Margate when her boss made her do a 'walk-and-talk' meeting around the town: step after step for four hours with Pearl 'trailing behind' as the hours went on. To get home, Pearl then had to walk four or five miles back to the train station because her boss claimed she couldn't find a taxi for her. The strain of that sort of physical excursion leads Pearl's muscles to tense ('It's hard to describe just how painful that is') and she had to spend the weekend in bed to recover. In the end, the trip was so damaging to her disability that it affected her posture for two months. By that point, only six weeks after starting the job, Pearl had already been fired – for what her employers termed 'creating a nega-tive atmosphere in the office'. 'Essentially, for getting publicly upset having been bullied because of my disability,' she translates.

In 2015, the Public Interest Research Unit (PIRU), with the campaign group Disabled People against Cuts (DPAC), catalogued the experiences of around 150 disabled workers, and found – as draconian assessments for out-of-work sick-ness benefits rolled out across the country – a 'disabled-scrounger' narrative permeated the workplace.[71] Disabled workers reported they were increasingly regarded as 'a burden', 'alien', 'lazy', or exaggerating their condition. One local authority worker, with a disability that affects his ability to walk, said his boss tried to make him move 'to a building with stairs and no lift'. Another, a shop worker with ADHD and obsessive–compulsive disorder on a zero-hours contract, spoke of being pressured to take extra shifts 'despite quoting the Disability [Discrimination] Act till I'm pink in the face'. While disabled people are dubbed 'lazy' for being unable to take on a job, to request support to make staying in work possible is vilified. As one public-sector worker with a neurological condition put it to the PIRU, even taking sick leave is viewed by bosses and colleagues as 'special treatment'.

It's this fear of being seen as 'trouble', Scope found in 2017, that meant that one in five disabled people do not disclose their disability to employers.[72] It's a gruelling way of working: pushing through pain in a meeting out of fear someone will see, or battling through fatigue in the toilets in case a colleague accuses you of skiving. Nearly half of disabled people have worried about 'coming out' as disabled to their employers, according to the same report.

This is not simply a case of outright hostility but sometimes something closer to 'benevolent prejudice'; that in-built belief among society that disabled people are simply less capable than 'normal' people. Analysis by Scope in 2014 found that nearly four in ten people thought of disabled people as less productive than non-disabled people, and 75 per cent of people thought of disabled people as 'needing to be cared for' some or most of the time. Over one in ten thought of disabled people as 'getting in the way' some or most of the time.[73] If an employer looks at a person with a crutch and sees them as needing to be looked after or an inconvenience, it's hard to imagine that worker is going to be hired or promoted.

Pearl is now challenging the decision of her dismissal and has sent her appeal letter to the chief executive of the media company. The process has exacerbated her anxiety, thus triggering her dystonia, causing more pain. She had moved back to London for the new job but now cannot afford to pay the rent and will have to move back in with her parents in Cardiff again 'unless I miraculously get a job'. 'I'm back to square one,' she says. 'I feel quite hopeless and depressed.'

In the spring of 2013, the workplace became that bit more insecure for disabled people. This was when the legal aid budget – the safety net for, among others, disabled people struck by discrimination at work – was gutted by £350 million a year amid vast changes to eligibility criteria. While since 2010 the 'welfare' budget has been lined up as the prime target for austerity, few government departments have remained immune to it. To that end, the coalition government issued sweeping changes to the legal aid system, excluding entire areas of law from the scope of legal aid under the guise of cost-cutting. While legal aid for housing rights was left with scraps, support for 'welfare' appeals and employment were decimated.

Overnight, a wheelchair user harassed as a 'scrounger' by her colleagues or an office manager sacked for developing depression was priced out of the legal system. In doing so, it marked the first change to fees since the tribunal system was established in 1964. In total, almost £1 billion was cut from the legal aid budget between 2010–11 and 2016–17, according to Ministry of Justice figures. By 2019–20, the Ministry of

Justice (MoJ) will have seen cuts to its overall budget of 40 per cent – among the deepest of any government department.[74] Before these changes, if someone like Pearl faced discrimination, they would have the protection of free legal support in order to help get justice. Now, to take a disability discrimination case to an employment tribunal, the individual has to find a minimum of £1,200 – or the equivalent of a couple of month's rent or half a year's worth of specialist food.

As it gutted legal aid funding, the government put what it termed 'an exceptional case' fund in place – an emergency safety net to, in theory, catch the most marginalized claimants. But to qualify for a reduced or no fee, an individual had to pass a monthly income and 'disposable-capital' test. It gives an insight into how well this protects disabled people that benefits like Disability Living Allowance (DLA) and its replacement, Personal Independence Payment (PIP), are actually judged as 'disposable capital' in these calculations, meaning that disabled applicants[75] – typically poorer and in need of DLA or PIP to pay for disability costs – are in the perverse situation of risking being judged as less eligible for help with fees than non-disabled people.

Unsurprisingly, since fees were introduced, disability discrimination claims have fallen rapidly: MoJ figures show that 63 per cent fewer claims were accepted by the employment tribunals between the first quarter of 2013–14 (pre-fees) and the first quarter of 2014–15 (post-fees).[76] By 2016, three years after the cuts to legal aid first came in, Amnesty International was declaring that a 'two tier' system had emerged: while the wealthy and, by extension, healthy could afford to buy access to justice, the poorest and ill were being shut out.[77]

Across the country, a desert of legal advice has been spreading in recent years. At the same time as legal aid was cut, local councils, squeezed by austerity to statutory services, pulled funding from welfare rights services, debt advice centres and law centres. The number of legal aid providers across England and Wales subsequently shrank by 20 per cent in just five years between 2012 and 2017,[78] while Citizens Advice and council-run advice centres shut their doors.

Put a pin in a map and each community has its story. The Law for All charity in Ealing, west London, closed as far back as 2011. West Norfolk's disability service, run by disabled people and their carers, began crowdsourcing in 2017 to stay afloat. There used to be nine law centres across Greater Manchester; now there are two. Out of a red-brick shop front in Manchester's Moss Side, the Greater Manchester Law Centre (GMLC), a pro bono centre run by volunteer barristers, trade union workers and law students, tries to fill the gap. By the time the GMLC officially opened its doors in February 2017, the team had already seen 200 cases. People started turning up as soon as they heard the centre was coming, knocking on the doors with plastic bags full of paperwork.

There's the rub, of course. It is not only that the government has pulled funding from legal aid or welfare advice centres, but that it did so at the same time as it brought in policies that mean that these services are needed more than ever. Stringent out-of-work tests falsely find disabled people 'fit for work' but local council cuts take away the welfare advice worker they can turn to for an appeal. Ministers' rhetoric of 'scrounging' disabled people fosters a discriminatory environment for disabled workers but changes to legal aid mean they likely can't afford to take their employer to court. While disabled people are increasingly perceived as having an 'easy life', the ultimate hostile climate has been crafted: pushed into any job by an adverse benefit system, made vulnerable to being victimized by employers, and cut off from the right to seek justice.

CHAPTER 3

Independence

On the worst nights, Rachel's wheelchair is her bed. The forty-four-year-old has arthritis of the spine and joints, on top of a string of other health conditions – fibromyalgia, Crohn's disease and Lupus – and since 2006 she has relied on a care package from her local council to enable her to live independently in a bungalow in the New Forest. But over the past eight years, as social care reductions have spread across the country, in Rachel's words, her care is 'just getting cut, cut, cut'.

In 2010, barely months after the coalition government gained power, Rachel's local authority stopped her visit from a care worker who helped her get ready for bed. Her cleaner and gardener went a few months later; cutbacks meant her council changed eligibility rules so only residents over the age of seventy could get the help. The following year, they pulled her evening care call too, meaning the end of her having a hot dinner. Rachel is often too weak to reach the oven from her wheelchair, and without a care assistant she can't cook herself a meal. By 2016, Rachel was left with just one forty-five-minute care slot a day: a morning visit to help her quickly get washed and dressed.

In May 2017, even this disappeared. Like many cash-strapped local councils, Rachel's social worker told her that if she wanted to keep even this provision, she would need to increase her contribution to her care costs. In fact, she would have to cover 90 per cent of it herself. That's £200 a fortnight – for barely a quarter of the care hours she started off with.

In theory, Rachel could use her disability benefits to cover some of the cost but in austerity's onslaught, nothing hits alone: the same month Rachel was handed her social care bill, she was transferred to the new Personal Independence Payment (PIP) – and promptly had her benefit cut. Rachel hasn't been able to earn a wage since the late 1990s – before becoming disabled, she worked as a nurse to the elderly – and with no way to pay her council's costs, she's had her support package entirely removed. 'I've no care at all now,' she says. 'Nothing.'

Look hard enough around Rachel's bungalow and you can see the signs. The lawn out the front has vanished – a friend dug it up and replaced it with gravel since there's no help to cut the grass. A group of teenagers from the local Scouts group trims the trees for her; 'Other than that, it'd be a jungle by now,' she explains. Indoors, the dust 'just builds up': months of having no one to keep it clean. Rachel bought a little 'robot hoover' to at least run over the bare floors. She makes jokes – 'It works as long as you don't run over it in your wheelchair,' she laughs – but the impact of having her social care removed is clearly brutal. As she puts it to me:

'I'm coping on my good days. On bad days, I don't get washed and dressed.'

If she's lucky, she says, she gets two 'good days' a week: spells where she can lift her arms out of her pyjamas in the morning or transfer herself out of her wheelchair and into a bed at night. To put that another way, with no care assistant to help her, for five days out of seven Rachel can't shower, get dressed or eat regular meals. To survive, on the days her arms are strong enough to lift a pot, she uses a slow cooker to build up a batch of meals for the week: stews and casseroles stored for when she physically cannot cook. Other days, she eats fruit or slices of bread.

Each month, Rachel goes to her GP for routine blood tests and over the past year, as the cuts took hold, she's been told she's now clinically malnourished. Her Crohn's disease already makes it harder for her to absorb nutrients but without a carer to help her cook, her body isn't even getting enough iron or vitamins to begin with. Instead, she's taking dissolvable vitamins from the chemist when she can. She struggles with sleep – sometimes she only gets a few hours stretched over the whole week – and as her pain increases, her energy shrinks.

This is Britain's social care system – where wheelchair users are left to become malnourished and sleeping in a bed is a luxury. In the years after the financial crash, as George Osborne kick-started the era of austerity, local councils were rapidly starved of cash from Westminster. It was local services – homelessness outreach services, libraries and children's centres – that took the hit, none more so than social care provision. Since 2010, adult social care has seen cuts of almost £6 billion, with the Local Government

Association (LGA) warning eight years later that care services for older and disabled adults were now 'on the brink of collapse'.

As social care began to hit the mainstream agenda in the post-2010 era, it became commonplace to hear ministers grilled on the subject of the ageing population or to read of elderly people subjected to the indignity of 'fifteen-minute' care slots. But as I heard more and more about this crisis, I began to notice something strange: disabled people like Rachel were largely missing from the picture. Listen to news coverage of social care and you will rarely hear the word 'disabled' uttered, just as you'll struggle to see a newspaper story on the 'care crisis' illustrated with a stock photo of someone below the age of seventy.

It's much the same in politics. When Theresa May addressed the House of Commons in December 2016 as the social care crisis began to gain attention, she pledged to ensure people would 'receive the care they needed in old age'[1] – as if there are not hundreds of thousands of disabled people who rely on the service throughout their lives.

Meanwhile, the government's long-delayed 2018 consultation on reforming the social care system failed to include a single disabled person or organization in the team of 'expert advisers'. In fact, while promising to work with services 'which help older people to live independently', working-age disabled people weren't addressed in the Green Paper at all.[2] After pressure, disability organizations were offered a 'round table discussion' instead. This sort of blackout is part of a wider exclusion of disabled people from the public consciousness and, with it, from media and politics. Just as the voices of those in poverty are largely absent from the national debate, the lives of disabled people are often distorted, marginalized or altogether ignored.

This has rarely been more blatant than in the social care debate. While disability is sidelined, disabled people actually represent a third of all social care users. That means around 400,000 working-age disabled people in England alone rely on a social care package[3] – say, a rotating team of personal assistants – to support them in their home with the tasks most take for granted. On paper, such packages enable basic human functions: getting to the toilet, cooking a meal or leaving the house for work. But really, they are much more than this – a way to gain control, dignity and, above all, a chance to live an independent life like anybody else.

There are now one million disabled people living without the social care they need, according to research by the charity Leonard Cheshire in November 2016.[4] That's equivalent to the population of Birmingham unable to get dressed in the morning or being housebound. Almost half the disabled people who say they need support told the charity they aren't receiving any at all. A separate study by Scope in 2015 painted a particularly harrowing picture of the social care system's treatment of disabled people.[5] The study found that over eight out of ten disabled people don't have enough social care hours, resulting in their being forced to sleep in their clothes, to go without washing or eating, or waiting fourteen hours to go the toilet. It sounds almost Victorian.

There are now widespread reports of disabled people like Rachel becoming physically sicker because they have no support to move or keep clean; or sliding into depression when, with no care worker to help them get out of the house, they are forced to spend all day and night within four walls.

Leonard Cheshire has found disabled people as young as their twenties being regularly forced into bed at 5 or 6 p.m. by their local authorities as, with stretched services, it's the only care slot available. Others are being told by their council to use incontinence pads and adult nappies – despite the fact that they're not incontinent – simply because there's no care worker to help them get to the toilet.

These funding cuts ushered into the social care system were so severe that, in 2017 when the United Nations issued its scathing report into the UK government's treatment of its disabled citizens, it highlighted what it dubbed the failure of the government 'to recognise the rights of disabled people to live independently in the community'.[6] In 2018, the Care and Support Alliance (CSA), a collection of eighty charities, warned that the care crisis had reached the point where disabled people were now having their legal 'rights breached'.[7] It found that a quarter of disabled people relying on social care had had their support cut between 2017 and 2018, despite their disabilities remaining the same or even worsening. Nearly half were subsequently now unable to leave the house, while a third couldn't maintain basic hygiene like washing or going to the toilet. A quarter had been forced to go without meals.[8]

As cash-strapped local authorities reeled from the shortfall in central government funding, disabled people like Rachel were increasingly expected to plug the gap themselves. While councils have always been legally entitled to charge for social care, in practice few asked individuals for anything but a small contribution, with others charging nothing at all. But with mounting financial pressure, recent years have seen a growing number of local authorities adopt or raise charges;

two-thirds of councils in England introduced or increased care fees between 2015 and 2018, according to the MS Society. In 2018, research by the union GMB found that more than 165,000 people were subsequently in what's dubbed 'social care debt' – in essence, being pushed into financial crisis.[9] Between 2016 and 2018, over 1,100 people were taken to court by local authorities;[10] wheelchair users hauled in front of a judge for needing social care but being too poor to pay for it. This picture is only set to get worse in the coming years. The LGA estimates that adult social care faces a £3.5 billion funding gap by 2025, with council's core funding in England set to be slashed by 77 per cent by 2020.[11]

In the New Forest, Rachel is becoming resigned to malnutrition – 'It's just going to happen now,' she says – and is focused simply on coping with no longer having any social care. 'Things might change,' she adds. 'If they stop badgering us disabled for once. Blaming us for everything.'

While care hours are cut, other council services are simultaneously pulled away. Take Meals on Wheels – an idea first born more than seventy years ago to counter wartime malnutrition and provide safety checks for isolated members of the community. In 2014, two-thirds of councils were offering a daily hot meal to help support disabled people and older residents in their own homes, according to the Association for Public Service Excellence.[12] Two years later, after half a decade of funding cuts, fewer than half of councils were still providing a Meals on Wheels service.[13]

Meanwhile, it's becoming increasingly common for the 'lifeline' service – an alarm that allows disabled and older people to call for help in an emergency – to come with a charge. Before the cuts, Rachel used to wear a chord around her wrist – a safety net connecting her to her care company and ambulance service. But in 2016, her council told her she'd have to start paying £100 a month for the privilege. 'They suddenly took it away,' she explains. When Rachel's heart isn't getting enough oxygen, she faints. Without her lifeline, nowadays, she'll wake up to find herself on the floor with no way to call for help. Instead, she has to slide herself across the floor and find a blanket to cover herself in. 'Then I reach my mobile to call a neighbour,' she says. When we speak again, a charity is helping Rachel train an assistance dog to act as her new alarm – philanthropy and a pet filling in the gaps where the state once was.

This shift to charity to plug the gaps of social care cuts is not an accident; it has been actively encouraged in recent years. In 2018, the government launched a new 'big society' – style strategy encouraging the public sector and charities to play 'a bigger role in the provision of public services', including social care.[14] Reminiscent of David Cameron's failed Big Society initiative launched in 2010 as cuts to public services began to bite, ministers pitched it not as a sign of government failure, but as a compliment to the British plucky spirit. In the words of the civil society strategy launch paper, 'All this is happening because of the resourcefulness of the British people.'[15]

Similar normalization of volunteerism is now commonplace. As the potential loss of EU migrants from Brexit began to hit, ministers warned in 2018 that women (notably, not men) might have to 'give up their jobs' to look after their ageing parents and disabled loved ones in the case of care worker shortages.[16] At the same time, a number of squeezed local councils admitted that if central government didn't step in with a long-term funding solution, they might not even be able to meet their legal duties, such as social care provision. East Sussex County Council, for example, stated that even services for 'vulnerable adults' could be 'unaffordable' by 2021, explaining that 'families and neighbourhood voluntary groups would have to take increasing responsibility' for supporting those people who would no longer qualify for social care.[17] It marks a blatant and unprecedented roll-back of the state.

The cultural image of a disabled person is traditionally helpless: at best a Tiny Tim–type brave figure, at worst a weak and passive individual, in need of being looked after by the non-disabled. It was a fitting rejoinder then that, just as with cuts to the 'welfare' budget, it has been disabled people at the forefront of the fight against social care reductions.

Take the Independent Living Fund (ILF) – a standalone fund issued by central government. This fund was the standard method over almost thirty years to help 18,000 of the most severely disabled people in the country to live in their own homes, work and be a part of the community by hiring personal assistants for their own care package. But in 2014, as a wave of austerity measures hit, the government announced it would be closing the £320 million fund and transferring all ILF's users to local authority social care provision. Unlike the ILF, the money would not be ring-fenced so there was no obligation for cash-strapped local councils to spend it on former ILF recipients rather than any other council duty – say, rubbish collections or potholes.

The politicians so keen to axe the fund were fully aware of

the consequences of their actions: half the local authorities that responded to the government's own ILF consultation said the move to local councils would result either in 'significantly reduced' care packages that would affect disabled people's ability to enjoy 'any quality of life', or in their being removed from their homes and put into residential care.[18] I reported on a protest outside the Department for Work and Pensions (DWP) headquarters in 2014 as angered ILF recipients lobbied with placards and chants. Scrawled on a makeshift cardboard prison cell wrapped around a protester's wheelchair, read the words: 'Without support, we become prisoners in our own homes.'

With protests came legal proceedings that went all the way to the High Court, as disabled campaigners fought through the courts for two years to save the ILF – and with it the principle that, even in tough economic times, disabled people in Britain have the right to independence. The court of appeal even quashed the government's first attempt to close the fund – finding that the DWP had given such little consideration to disabled people's right to equality and 'ability to take part in public life' that it actually breached the Equality Act.[19]

In the end, however, despite legal and direct action, the ILF was axed in 2015;[20] within months, its former users across the country – now solely reliant on their local councils – began to have their care packages cut.[21] Two years later, in the summer of 2017, disabled activists used their wheelchairs to block the MPs' entrance to the House of Commons, demanding the restoration of the Independent Living Fund.[22] The chant went out: 'This is a message to Theresa May – while we have no justice, you will have no peace.'

Historically, disabled people in Britain were deprived of the right to live independently. Throughout the last century, we were routinely housed in out-of-town institutions, from schools for Deaf and blind people, and lifelong care facilities, to mental asylums. The term sometimes used to describe this – 'warehousing' – creates an image of the dehumanization at work here: disabled people stored under one roof as a way to reduce the costs of their care. This was often said to be for 'their own good' and for the good of the rest of the public, with disabled citizens segregated from a non-disabled society that saw them as freaks, burdens or shameful secrets to hide away. Though this was often a private arrangement within a family, it was approved by the heart of the British establishment; for example, in 1913 the Mental Incapacity Act passed, seeing 40,000 men and women locked away on grounds of their being 'feeble-minded' or 'morally defective'.[23]

In her 2010 New Statesman essay 'When the disabled were segregated', journalist Victoria Brignell describes vividly what life was like in these institutions.[24] She recounts how, at one facility in the 1950s, patients with mental health problems could only have one bath a week and toilets only had half-doors so people's feet and heads were visible. At another, patients were not allowed out and could not have visitors. If they wet themselves, they were punished. Staff would physically assault patients in the toilets at night. Others recounted being banned from wearing their own clothes and instead having to help themselves from one large cupboard on the ward.

This sort of dehumanizing practice towards disabled residents was standard, with some institutions adopting humiliating practices as part of their admissions process. Brignell recounts how one care home for people with learning disabilities used to forcibly cut young women's hair when they arrived. If residents put up resistance, they were tied to a chair while the cutting took place and then locked in a dark room for up to half an hour before being injected with drugs.

As I grew up as a disabled teenager planning a life of university, a career and my own home, such horror stories appeared relics of the distant past, a world away from the disability equality I was repeatedly told now existed in my country. But there was not as much space between us as I had hoped. The institutionalization of disabled people was common in Britain as recently as the 1970s and continued until the early 1980s, barely a couple of years before I was born. Those who escaped this fate were often still not afforded the chance to live independently, but were instead largely left to languish at home into adulthood with their families, seeing out the decades in their childhood bedrooms.

Over the next forty years, disabled campaigners fought for the basic right to independent living. Against a culture that largely viewed disabled people as children to be cared for, or dehumanized as objects to be put away, the independent-living movement in Britain fought for disabled people to be treated as ordinary adults, with the same rights to freedom, dignity and choice as anyone else. It was throughout the 1970s that this battle really took hold. While legislation such as the Chronically Sick and Disabled Persons Act 1970 – dubbed 'a Magna Carta for the disabled'[25] – for the first time required local authorities to provide disabled people with support in their own homes, and equipment, it was pressure from RADAR (the Royal Association for Disability Rights), a leading disability organization formed in the 1970s to remove the barriers facing disabled people, that further fought for these rights to be implemented. They set up advocacy support in the 1980s to help disabled people get the care they were entitled to.

The UK's first Centre for Independent Living was opened in 1984 and over the subsequent decades, scores of such organizations were born, each run by disabled people, employing disabled people, and providing the practical and campaigning support to enable thousands to live independently, as well as tackle other basic needs such as housing, access, employment and education. By the mid-1990s, the Community Care (Direct Payments) Act had launched the first use of direct payments – the groundbreaking scheme that enables disabled people to organize their own social care rather than the local council – while the introduction of the Care Act in England in 2015 placed local authorities under the powerful obligation of providing a care package that 'promotes' an individual's well-being.

That this battle had its origins as recently as forty years ago simultaneously shows both how fragile Britain's disabled people's gains are and creates the illusion that we're currently experiencing a heyday for disability equality. In reality, we are witnessing a piecemeal dismantling of disabled people's right to independence, in which our freedom is sold to the highest bidder. Passing the Care Act at the same time as launching unprecedented cuts to social care meant that the promise to 'promote' disabled people's 'well-being' resulted in the opposite.

A third of disabled people say the level of choice and control they enjoyed over their support has actually 'reduced or reduced significantly' since the Care Act came in, according to research by charity In Control.[26] Well over half (58 per cent) say their quality of life has 'reduced or reduced significantly' in the past year, with many describing how the hours of work or volunteering that they used to be able to do had been shrunk and others reporting that their support was now restricted to personal care;[27] that's a life steered around toilet visits but no help to see a friend in the pub. Linda Burnip, co-founder of the campaign group Disabled People against Cuts, puts it frankly to me: 'These cuts are rolling the right to independent living back decades.'

'Independent living' is in many ways a political euphemism for control – the right for disabled people to have the same choices over our own life as anyone else. Yet as budgets were cut to the bone, I began to hear from more and more disabled people who were being forced into rigid care packages by their councils or local healthcare provider, the clinical commissioning group (CCG). They told me of horrific results: such as a group of young men with cerebral palsy in supported housing who reported being made to 'share care' – literally, share care hours and assistants between them – because they live under one roof. Brothers with a muscle-wasting disease described to me how they were unable to go to university because they were given one care package between them; due to the fact their shared personal assistants can only be in one place at a time, if one brother went to lectures, the other would have to as well.

There is no starker example of this than the post-2010 drive to move disabled people back into care homes. While Britain appears to have progressed from the days of 'warehousing' disabled adults in institutions, a cocktail of cuts to social care and the NHS teamed with a lack of accessible housing options means that recent years have seen a number of disabled people quietly moved out of their homes and into residential care, with thousands of others threatened with a similar move.

As funding for care was hacked in 2017, a new funding cap was rolled out in at least forty-four CCGs; in essence, creating an 'upper limit' on the amount of money spent on care in a person's home, even if it's not sufficient to meet their care needs.[28] Continuing healthcare can be arranged in a care home, a nursing home, a hospice or a person's own home. But new funding caps meant that many disabled people could suddenly be prevented from living at home with their families despite being well enough to do so. By 2018, disabled people were already receiving warnings from CCGs that if they couldn't live on the newly capped funding for their home support, they would be moved into residential care.

This is as alarming as it sounds: one day, a forty-something woman is living in her own bungalow with her husband, and the next she's put in a care home with strangers. The EHRC warned in 2017 that this cost-cutting means that disabled people in the UK face being 'interned' in care homes, in what amounts to a potential breach of their human rights.[29] Less than a year later, a dozen NHS organizations faced legal action over what the EHRC called 'discriminatory' policies around pushing disabled people into residential care.[30]

As local government had its budgets squeezed, disabled people who receive care funding from their local council rather than CCG began to find themselves in a similar position. It is legal for local authorities to take use of resources into account, as well as peoples' choices and needs, meaning that when an individual's home care gets to the same price as, or is more expensive than, a residential care home, councils are allowed to look at alternatives.

For a minority, a care home can be a suitable arrangement they have chosen, but for many others it is a nightmare, one that is born not from a free choice of what's best for the individual but is the result of cost-cutting imposed by council officials. As one young disabled woman fighting to stay in her own home put it to me, 'It's terrifying. A stranger that's never met me can make a decision about my life.' Shipping off disabled people into care homes is the inescapable consequence of a political climate that puts a price tag on certain people's lives and, at the same time, fans the belief that disabled people are a cost that the so-called hardworking taxpayer shouldn't have to pay.

At only thirty, Pete was forced to move into a care home. He has cerebral palsy and scoliosis of the spine, and uses an electric wheelchair. For eight years, he lived independently with the support of personal assistants in a flat he owns in Portsmouth. The council provided him with funding for twelve hours' support each day. 'Slowly but surely they cut it back,' he says. By 2016, his care package was reduced to just four visits a day. That entitled him to help with getting up, someone to make him lunch, another to make him dinner, and being helped to bed. With the new skeleton care package, he had no help to get out of the flat to see friends, while being left alone for hours at a time led to his health deteriorating.

Hernia of the oesophagus means Pete needs anti-sickness tablets before each meal – he has a tube inserted directly into the stomach because he can't take medication by mouth. But the cuts to his care means he no longer has anyone to help him with it. 'After each visit I was feeling sick all day when they'd gone and the only thing I could do was going to hospital because it was safe,' he says. 'I was frightened of choking on my own vomit.'

Living like that, Pete says, was like 'being in limbo': he was still in his flat but he was repeatedly going in and out of hospital because of the toll of social care cuts on his health. Pete asked the council for more care slots but he was turned down; he was told four slots are the maximum anyone could have because of their squeezed budget. On paper, disabled people such as Pete are still being afforded the right to live in their own home, but in reality the care is cut to such a thread-bare level that remaining there has become impossible.

In the end, Pete felt so unsafe in his flat without an adequate social care package that he had to take the drastic move of accepting a place at a care home. In fact, Pete was placed in a residential care home designed for the elderly. 'I'm the only one here that's young,' he says. This is far from rare. A Freedom of Information request submitted by the MS Society and Care and Support Alliance (CSA) in 2017 found that 3,300 working-age disabled people in England are living in care homes for the elderly.[31] The MS Society found that reasons ranged from there being no accessible housing in the community; the disabled person being unable to afford, or to access grants, to adapt their own inaccessible home; to older people's homes being seen as the only place available in the area to adequately meet their complex health needs.

Pete has no complaints about the care home – 'The care is exemplary,' he says – and he's relieved staff 'allowed me to have Sky in my room' to watch football. 'I'm a massive Pompey fan,' he says. But it's hard not to feel anger that for years he has lived in his own home but, simply due to care cuts, he's now had his independence taken. 'It's just so disappointing you can't get this level of care in the community any more because of the government cuts,' he says. 'In the future I can see no disabled person living independently and us all being in care homes regardless of our age.'

With little hope of things changing, now thirty-one, Pete tells me he's had to put his flat on the market. 'I wish I was in my own place still but I have to look after my own health,' he says. 'The government may take away my flat but they're not taking away my health and dignity.'

It says something about the situation facing disabled people that, in some ways, Pete counts himself lucky. His independence is gone but he is at least at a care home in which he's treated well. This is often not the case; as employers struggle to retain care staff on low wages and increasingly heavy workloads, research by the Care Support Alliance (CSA), a coalition of more than 80 charities, in 2018 found one in five care residents had gone without meals and a quarter had gone without basic needs such as washing, getting dressed and going to the toilet.[32] One respondent said they had not been washed for more than two months and that their pyjamas had not been changed all year.

This institutionalization is particularly prevalent for people with learning disabilities – increasing the potential threat of neglect and abuse. Recent years have seen multiple cases of abuse at care homes in Britain hit the headlines. In October 2012, six care workers at Winterbourne View care home, south Gloucestershire, were given prison terms for 'cruel, callous and degrading' abuse of disabled people.[33] In a high-profile BBC *Panorama* investigation, workers were filmed slapping residents with severe learning disabilities, soaking them in water, trapping them under chairs, taunting and swearing at them, pulling their hair and poking their eyes. Five years on, more than a dozen directors and staff at two care homes in Devon were convicted for the 'organised and systematic' abuse of disabled residents: people with learning disabilities held in empty rooms without food, heating or a toilet.[34] The prosecution likened the conditions to 'training an animal'.

While the extremes of Winterbourne View far from represents all residential care, this is not simply a case of a few bad apples. In 2018, on what was the largest-ever survey of care home staff in England, University College London found that abuse was taking place in at least some form in 99 per cent of care homes due to 'chronic underfunding'.[35] The most common abusive behaviours were making someone wait for care or not giving them sufficient time to be able to eat. A minority reported verbally and physically assaulting residents.

Such abuse is a particularly brutal example of where dehumanization of disabled people in the UK has led to – of how long-standing prejudice that sees disabled people as different, objects, or burdens, has combined with austerity to see us treated as if we are less than human. As cuts to disability services kicked in after the global crash, the same dehumanization that made it 'permissible' to starve a wheelchair user through benefit cuts encouraged a belief that locking up disabled people in institutions after removing their social care was somehow acceptable.

More than this, it stoked the idea that this was perfectly normal. Wouldn't disabled people be better off in a care home? After all, they need to be cared for and this way they can all get the help they need. As I researched this subject after 2010, I began to hear this argument more and more. 'Why not put them all in one place?' was a common response from members of the public when I wrote about social care changes. Others professed a desire to help but relented due to what they saw as financial constraints: 'It's awful for disabled people but how expensive is 24/7 care for all of them?'

Ethics aside, this argument ignores the economics at work. The Women's Budget Group has shown that if you invest 2 per cent of GDP in the care sector, you get double the number of jobs compared to investment in construction.[36] Meanwhile, supporting disabled people enables many to work themselves and in turn pay taxes. It's telling, then, that the argument that decent provision for disabled people is too costly is actually fatally flawed, but more worrying still is that disabled people's lives are seen in these cold mathematical terms. It's a hop, skip and jump to pulling out a spreadsheet and calmly calculating how much exactly a disabled life is worth. In this climate, the truly reasonable are the ones arguing to round up the disabled from their living rooms and put us in institutions.

When Sue lost her right leg in 2014, she was already close to being housebound. The fifty-seven-year-old had multiple health problems, including osteoarthritis in each of her joints. Chronic vascular disease accounts for the wheelchair, two sticks, crutches and seated walker filling the flat. Over the following two years, Sue had nine operations – the last a leg amputation right up to the hip. Her 'good' leg – ravaged with a sort of burning pins and needles – meant she struggled daily. In addition, she has chronic obstructive pulmonary disease (COPD); in layman's terms, her lungs can't empty the air she needs.

There are grab rails throughout the flat to help her move from one room to the next. 'Sometimes I can go a whole week without falling. Others it's three to four times a week,' she says. But thanks to Motability – the government-backed scheme that enables some severely disabled people to lease a suitable vehicle in exchange for their disability benefit – Sue was still able to get out and about when she wanted.

Sue speaks to me from Blackley, a few miles north of the centre of Manchester. Her local Tesco Metro is both her primary stop for food and the crux of her old meticulous routine. She'd drive her Motability car the few minutes there, park directly outside with her blue badge, use her walker to get from the car park, borrow one of the store's scooters to pick up a few bits, and then drive home. The car, she explains, was adapted. A flip foot-pedal adaptation and automatic gears. It meant she could still drive where she needed even with her amputation and deteriorating health – and all for the price of part of her Disability Living Allowance (DLA).

Established in 1978, for three decades the Motability scheme has provided this service for millions of disabled people, enabling them to swap their disability benefits for the lease of a car, scooter or powered wheelchair. As of 2018, it bought and sold 200,000 cars each year.[37] In many ways, it's the definition of an efficient fund, overcoming two hurdles in one: it provides transport to citizens who need a vehicle in order to get around, and who – due to being more likely to be in poverty as well as often unable to access public transport – may otherwise be cut off from buying one themselves.

For many disabled people, it's more than a mundane government policy. It's a piece of independence: the only way to get to work, see friends or go to the shops. But when the coalition abolished DLA in 2013 and replaced it with the notoriously tougher PIP, Motability users like Sue suddenly found themselves having to reapply to keep their own car, in effect going through a new assessment in order to keep the lifeline they've relied on for years.

Under burgeoning austerity, the Motability scheme had in many ways become the poster child of the 'disabled-benefit-scrounger' narrative: a tangible patsy for the idea that, while 'hardworking' families struggled to make ends meet in the post-crash economy, it was only logical to be suspicious of your disabled neighbour when he drives by your house in a new car. In June 2011, under the headline 'Free BMWs for pals of disabled in scam', the *Sun* ran a story alleging that 'THOUSANDS of people are enjoying luxury Mercedes and BMW cars provided free by the taxpayer,'[38] peddling the myth that huge numbers are faking disability in order to milk a car from the state. Five years later, right-wing newspapers were still spreading this propaganda: in June 2016, the *Daily Mail* was warning readers how 'thousands are driving off in vehicles paid for by YOU' as it detailed how the Motability scheme was supposedly frittering away £2 billion of taxpayers' money.[39] As its baiting headline dubbed it: 'The car scam that will drive you crackers.'

If it's a scam, Sue is an Oscar-worthy actor. When she was tested for PIP in September 2016, she was so ill that the assessors had to let her have a rare home visit: she answered the questions sat in her wheelchair, wearing pyjamas, and with her prosthetic leg off. Still, she was rejected for PIP. Sue had been on DLA for a decade but, just like that, she was informed she'd been kicked off the Motability scheme.

After the assessment, the consequences followed swiftly: Sue had twelve weeks to return her car and hand over the keys to the dealer. By Christmas, like thousands of others, the car had gone back to the garage, complete with its adaptations for Sue's amputation. By 2018, over 75,000 disabled people across Britain had lost their cars, power wheelchairs and scooters due to benefit changes according to Motability figures; that's over 40 per cent of all clients.[40] Over the following years, as the PIP assessments continue to roll out, this is set to only increase.

For all its politics, the result is simple and brutal for Sue: 'It means being housebound. Without the car, I'm stuck.' Buses arrive regularly 300 metres down the bottom of her road but that means little when you're not able to get to the bus stop. Walking a few metres is filled with nausea and pain for Sue. When her osteoarthritis flares up in bad weather, her joints lock up, and sometimes her stump is too sore to tolerate her prosthetic leg. Her breathlessness means she can't self-propel her wheelchair that far. Suddenly, without the car, she could not do even the most basic things like getting out to pay a bill, 'or buy bread and milk,' she says.

Research by the Disability Benefit Consortium, a national coalition of over eighty charities and disability organizations, found in 2017 that four in ten disabled people say the transfer to PIP has led them to become more isolated.[41] Over a

quarter of disabled people say they aren't even able to get to
medical appointments any more.[42] With no car, Sue had to
start using NHS 'private transport' to get to the hospital to
see her consultants; sometimes half a dozen times a month.
It's the sort of economic incompetence that's become central
to 'welfare reform': take back an already adapted car only for
stretched NHS budgets to have to provide more expensive
transport.

The Motability scheme is not without its troubles. In
2018, a report by the government spending watchdog, the
National Audit Office (NAO), criticized the company for its
high financial reserves and top executive pay, citing the £1.7
million earned by the scheme's chief executive, Mike Betts.[43]
Within a few weeks of the report, Betts had resigned, though
not before receiving a £2.2 million bonus on top of his
seven-figure salary.[44] The backlash was warranted. A chief
exec of a disability charity making millions in many ways
spoke to the worst of Britain's inequality and bloated fat cat
culture. But it is telling how much coverage it received from
politicians and sections of the press compared to the loss of
cars by disabled people. Moreover, the very same ministers
who queued up to criticize Motability out of apparent
concern for disabled clients were often the ones responsible
for the policy that was removing their cars from them. When
the House of Commons debated Motability's executive pay
in February 2018, then welfare chief Esther McVey was
accused of making a series of untrue claims about the
Motability Scheme, effectively using the pay scandal as an
opportunity to try and shift the blame from her own department's benefit cuts. This included urging the charity's trus-
tees to be 'held to account' after another MP described how

a constituent had been threatened with having her lifelong Motability vehicle removed on Boxing Day – when in fact it was the government's benefits policy that meant she was deemed no longer eligible for the car.[45]

To have a chance at getting back her right to a car, Sue applied for help from Fightback4Justice – one of the pro bono legal groups patching the gaps of dwindling welfare rights and legal centres. In some ways, she was lucky as she at least found a volunteer to help her through the process. In 2018, it emerged that 99 per cent of disabled people had been deprived of support for benefit appeals since 2011 due to the introduction of legal aid cuts.[46] Still, it would be difficult to say Sue had 'luck'. While she was appealing, her health rapidly deteriorated: in May 2017, she was diagnosed with terminal rectal cancer. Only two months later, in the middle of cancer treatment, Sue had to make her way to a tribunal in the city centre. The decision was almost instantaneous, she says: 'We walked in. They said, "We can't understand why they've taken it off you." They gave it back.'

It took another two months after her appeal for Sue to actually get a car back. Her old specially adapted car had long gone so she had to order a new one, get it delivered to the dealer, and then the dealer send the car to an adaptations company. Five days after we last spoke, Sue picked up a new car: a bright yellow Nissan Juke. 'I looked through the book and thought, "sod it, I'll get one that gets me noticed," ' she says. 'They call it "Sunshine Yellow." '

It took a year-long battle to get here; to get back to where she started. In the process, she's had to use her limited time left fighting, while also stuck in her flat, housebound. As we talk, she uses an inhaler – a spray into her mouth each time her breath catches. She tells me she's pledging to use every day she has left, though she can't get back what she lost. She pauses: 'It took my independence off me.'

Without a wheelchair, three months can pass without Philomena leaving her terrace house in Liverpool. The fifty-three-year-old has multiple chronic illnesses – heart disease, double incontinence and chronic fatigue – and each makes it hard for her to physically move. COPD, on top of heart disease, means she gets breathless when she walks. Her right leg throbs from cardiovascular disease and fibromyalgia causes burning pain. She can make it around thirty feet on crutches – about the length of three cars – before the pain kicks in. 'The pain is horrendous, even to get to my neighbours. I can't walk anywhere.'

Still, after asking the NHS for four years for a wheelchair, she's been repeatedly turned down for help. 'Everyone just says, "there's no money for wheelchairs." Like you can magic one [yourself] out of nowhere.'

Ask a member of the British public and the impression is often that if a disabled person needs a wheelchair, the state will provide one. In 2017, YouGov polling commissioned by spinal chord charity Back Up found that this belief was so ingrained that 60 per cent of UK adults believed that people who need a wheelchair should only have to wait up to one month, or should be given one straight away.[47] But listen to Philomena describe her life and you soon get a clue of just how far this is from reality.

It's local GP-led services, CCGs, across the country that determine the policy and budgets for wheelchairs in each area, but just like with social care, as austerity heavily reduced funding, this service has been hit. When Philomena asked her GP for help, she was told that the NHS was 'hard-pressed at the moment' and that her CCG didn't have funding for a wheelchair. Instead, Adult Social Services provided her with a trolley – something to lean on and put food and drinks in as she pushes it around the house. When she asked her occupational therapist, she said there 'wasn't any money for wheelchairs' and suggested Philomena buy her own.

That's easier said than done. A suitable wheelchair often costs at least £2,000, with the most specialist as much as £25,000. For a family with health problems, this is beyond expensive. It is a class issue as much as a disability one; while richer families will be able to find several thousands of pounds to buy a wheelchair, those on a low income will find it impossible on top of rent, utilities and food (households that are already much more likely to be living in poverty due to disability).

Philomena hasn't been well enough to earn a wage since the 1990s, when she worked in a local off-licence. Her husband, a public sector tax worker, hasn't had a pay rise for a decade. Once the two of them pay all the bills, they usually save for treats for their seven-year-old granddaughter – 'A pound here. A fifty pence there.' At that rate, if Philomena spent the money on herself, it would take her around 160 years to have enough for a basic wheelchair.

Philomena represents what is a widespread crisis of disabled people in Britain being left without wheelchairs. The NHS wheelchair charter, which was drawn up by campaigners before being adopted by NHS England, states that access and provision should be equal for all, 'irrespective of age or postcode', but it's common practice for people to languish for years on waiting lists or to be turned down entirely. A BuzzFeed investigation into wheelchair provision on the NHS in 2017 found almost a quarter of people referred by GPs to wheelchair services are not being given any equipment at all.[48] It also uncovered an extreme 'postcode lottery': in some parts of the UK, disabled people are provided with the right chair, but in others, three-quarters of those referred are offered nothing by wheelchair services.[49]

On top of this, it confirmed there are large delays in disabled people getting help: 96 per cent of areas are missing their target to supply all wheelchairs within the eighteen weeks guaranteed by the NHS constitution.[50] Even children aren't guaranteed care by the state. Analysis in the *Health Service Journal* (*HSJ*) in 2018 showed that over 5,000 disabled children in England who need a wheelchair are waiting more than the four-month target for the equipment to be delivered, resulting in children struggling to go to school or be rehabilitated.[51]

Wheelchairs are rarely seen in positive terms by non-disabled people. Flick through a media report mentioning a disabled person with mobility problems and the phrase used is typically 'wheelchair-bound' – as if the wheelchair has contained the individual and they are stuck helpless in the corner of the room. When Stephen Hawking died in 2018, cartoons and imagery used by many media outlets spoke of him being 'free' of his wheelchair, with death seemingly a fortunate escape from the wheels and metal that 'trapped' a great mind. In fact, this is far from the truth.

While cultural perceptions of disability perpetuate the idea that wheelchairs are prisons, for disabled people like Philomena they represent freedom: the only way to see family, meet a friend or do everyday things. 'It'd be nice to say, "Let's go to the shops,"' she explains. She recently saw a Batgirl outfit on Asda's website for her great-niece – a little tutu – and a friend suggested they go and look at it in person. She hasn't been to Asda for almost a year, she tells me. She can't. 'I'm stuck in the house 24/7.'

This sort of isolation is a common consequence of poor wheelchair provision, including for those who only need one short term. The British Red Cross warned in 2018 that a UK-wide shortage of wheelchairs was leaving as many as 4 million people a year housebound and isolated, some of whom are terminally ill and are spending the last few months of their life trapped at home.[52]

When I next speak to Philomena, it's the day after a rare trip outside to the opticians. Without a wheelchair, she had to walk with crutches, a portable nebulizer sitting in her handbag for when she got out of breath. She was soon paying for it: as she got home, she put her crutches down and sat on the stairs, and her husband had to help her straight to bed. Today, she can 'barely walk'. Her arms are burning; legs 'killing' her. 'I feel like I've been run over by a bus.' It will take her days to get over the leg pains, but she tells me she's got a hospital appointment tomorrow. Her husband – himself recovering from a stroke – tries to reassure her, saying, 'we'll just have to hope the hospital's got a wheelchair available.' 'If my husband wasn't there, I wouldn't even be able to push round the ward,' she says.

Each day, Philomena lives with what you might call tantalizing independence. Even with council cuts to bus services, there's decent public transport on her road; as she puts it, 'I'm well connected to the buses . . . if I could get to the bus stop.' Her housing association put in a handrail on the outside door of the house and widened the steps so she could use it with her crutches. But without a wheelchair, she can't physically make it past the bottom of her road. 'It's like living in the Victorian times,' she says. 'We're locked away so no one knows we exist.'

It's hard to feel that this isn't the definition of a nation's literal hidden shame: disabled people trapped behind closed doors because, if you can't walk, the state still won't provide a wheelchair. Disabled people in Britain have long had to live without wheelchairs. Despite being born with a disability, I didn't get my first wheelchair until I was ten. Before then, I got around in a large buggy that, in the 1990s, health services thought was the best way to transport a growing child on the way to secondary school. In the end, my parents got help from a charity, Whizz-kidz, to afford a suitable wheelchair.

But in recent years, it feels as if this situation has got worse. As cuts to the social care and social security system chip away at disabled people's independence, squeezed budgets mean that CCGs are increasingly turning down people like Philomena for wheelchairs. Some will only provide a basic wheelchair – rather than one that's suitable and safe for an individual's disability. Others who used to offer 'vouchers' – in essence, a scheme that allowed CCGs to contribute a small sum towards a chair – have scrapped them.

This situation has quietly reached such dire straits that in June 2017, medics at the British Medical Association's annual representative meeting in Bournemouth unanimously passed a motion calling for users to have 'timely access to chairs suitable for their individual conditions'.[53] It perhaps gives a hint of the lack of priority given to disabled people's lives that there's little information on what help wheelchair users are actually receiving: there aren't national eligibility criteria for receiving mobility equipment and until 2015 there wasn't even centrally gathered data on wheelchair services across the country.

Philomena makes dark jokes about how fraught she is – 'I say to my GP, *can't you just cut my leg off? Least then I'd get a wheelchair*' – but this desperation is real. In recent years, I've spoken to a number of disabled people who have resorted to buying a cheap wheelchair on the Internet after being rejected by NHS wheelchair services. One student told me she spent £50 on an untested wheelchair from Amazon because she had no other option. She went on to incur permanent injuries.

The wrong wheelchair can be as damaging as none at all: research by ComRes on behalf of the Toyota Mobility Foundation in 2018 found that 90 per cent of wheelchair users in the UK have experienced pain and discomfort as a result of their mobility devices.[54] Others are turning to crowdfunding to raise money for a suitable chair, where having to ask strangers for help on the Internet is akin to the modern day 'cripple with a begging bowl'.

Crowdfunding websites, such as Kickstarter and JustGiving, are best known for allowing people to raise money for their own personal cause: a community project or a school club. But cuts to services means they're increasingly being used to fulfil what's a serious medical need; the amount of money raised for wheelchairs on JustGiving increased fourfold between 2015 and 2016, from £365,000 to £1.8 million.[55] Philomena says a friend suggested she set up a GoFund page but she couldn't bring herself to. 'No,' she says, adamantly. 'Asking a stranger for money. We weren't brought up that way.'

The issue of wheelchair provision is likely to become increasingly pressing in the coming years. From 2018 all CCGs in England began replacing the existing wheelchair voucher scheme with personal wheelchair budgets, in which people are told up-front how much money is available for their wheelchair, based on an assessment of their individual needs and goals. And yet this is happening at a time of vast cuts in resources. In addition to wider NHS funding pressures, other limited avenues for wheelchair funding are pulled away, from cuts to Access to Work – the fund that pays for practical support for disabled people at work – to tightened eligibility for the Motability scheme, which provides, as well as cars, powered wheelchairs in exchange for benefits.

Philomena used to be on a 'lifetime award' of disability benefits until the reforms set in a couple of years ago. She had double pleurisy during the assessment – 'I could hardly breathe from the pain,' she says – but regardless, the officials cut it. She used to use her disability benefit to help run a car – petrol and insurance costs – but since her benefit's been cut, she's had to give that up.

With no car or wheelchair, Philomena is clear about the consequences: 'They took my little bit of independence.' As we finish talking, she tells me that she and her husband are currently saving to take their granddaughter and daughter to a local theme park day: grandparents go free and other tickets are fourteen pounds. Most importantly, wheelchairs are provided without charge. 'Just a day out with Nanny,' she says. 'She'll just be glad Nanny's out.'

CHAPTER 4

Housing

For the last six years, Robert has been trapped in an attic flat in Brighton. The thirty-four-year-old has tetraplegia due to a degenerative neurological disease – his body is almost fully paralysed except for his lower left arm. But when he applied for social housing in 2012, due to a lack of accessible properties in the area, his council assigned him a second-floor flat – with no lift access. Back then, Robert's condition hadn't advanced enough for him to need a wheelchair but he was already unable to walk up stairs – 'My legs would collapse from under me' – and with two flights of stairs to the attic, there was no way for him to get in or out of the flat. Still, Robert had no choice but to accept the property: he was living in a homeless shelter at the time and with no other options from the council and his paralysis spreading, he had nowhere else to go.

Since then, the flat has become a prison. Robert now needs a wheelchair full-time, but because there's no lift, he's stuck inside. Before he got ill, Robert ran his own interior design company, was a keen gardener, and could be found most days and nights at the gym or out dancing. Accessible housing would have enabled him to keep at least some aspects of his former life but, instead, he's lost it all. He has no contact with his old friends. He goes outside so rarely that he's developed a severe vitamin D deficiency from the lack of sunlight. The only time he leaves his flat is to go to the hospital, he says. 'The highlights of my life these days are my [medical] appointments . . . when I get to see what the outside world looks like again.'

To achieve this, he goes through a sort of torture: to get out of the flat, one of his personal assistants slowly pulls him down the stairs. It takes about two hours to do it – one step at a time, his body physically dragged over two flights of narrow stairs. Often, Robert falls. His paralysis means he hasn't got the strength in his back to hold himself up, so, as his assistant tries to pull him carefully, he slips. Ask him about the injuries he's had from this and it's an endless list: a smashed shoulder, knee, head. A sprained wrist. He can't feel his legs any more, he adds, so he can't feel what damage he's done there.

Being paralysed in an attic flat not only means Robert has no way to get out of his home. He can't safely move inside it either. His wheelchair sits chained up at the bottom of the stairs: he has no way to get it up the stairs or move it through the cramped rooms and doorways of the tiny flat. Instead, to get around his home, Robert is dragged: he sits on the floor, his personal assistant puts his arm, under his torso, and he's pulled from one room to the next. 'Like a piece of meat,' he says.

It's well established that recent years have seen Britain enter a housing crisis, with rising house prices and rents at a time of stagnating wages seeing the secure, affordable homes enjoyed by previous generations becoming increasingly out of reach. The issue has received vast political and media attention, in which politicians from all sides utter commitments to house building while news items chronicle the lives of families forced to save for years for a deposit and yet still find themselves shut out of the housing market. But for disabled people like Robert, this crisis is altogether starker.

In 2018, the Equality and Human Rights Commission released its findings of an eighteen-month inquiry into accessible housing in Britain, finding what it called a 'chronic shortage' of suitable homes for disabled people.[1] The inquiry reported disabled people being trapped inside their homes, or having to eat, sleep and bathe in one room. Others spoke of how they had to be carried around their homes by family members; grown adults 'piggybacked' up to their bed. As I began to talk to disabled people about their housing over the last few years, I found a similar picture: a wheelchair user washing in a paddling pool in his kitchen with a hose because he couldn't use his bathroom. A mother falling down concrete steps carrying her son's wheelchair. A young woman forced to use a commode in the living room because the toilet was upstairs.

According to research by the London School of Economics (LSE) for the charity Papworth Trust in 2016, there are 1.8 million disabled people struggling to find accessible housing.[2] Leonard Cheshire estimates that as many as one in six disabled adults and half of all disabled children live in housing that is not suitable for their needs.[3] This is not surprising when you consider how few properties are accessible: in England, a staggering 93 per cent of housing stock is inaccessible to disabled people, as it fails to meet minimum accessibility standards.[4]

That homes in Britain are almost exclusively designed for non-disabled people cannot be seen in isolation. When it comes to infrastructure of any type – whether that is shops, restaurants, transport or sporting venues – the default setting is 'non-disabled', with public and private buildings alike aimed at people who can walk up steps rather than require a ramp. This failure to implement equal access to housing, transport, and social venues is so severe that in 2016 the EHRC said it amounts to treating disabled people like 'second-class citizens'.[5] On a practical level, when much of Britain's housing stock was built, disability access was decades away from being a legal requirement. The friends' homes that I could not enter throughout my childhood in Lincolnshire – say, a Victorian terrace house – were built during a time in which the idea of someone with a disability wanting a home of their own would have seemed preposterous. The right to an accessible home – and, with it, a certain level of independence and freedom – hardly fits with a society that had next to no expectation that disabled people might ever have a family or income of their own or even be part of society.

But if the lack of access of old homes can be excused as 'a sign of the times', the lack of progress in twenty-first-century Britain is surely also reflective of a modern indifference. The same 'non-disabled' default that sees shops or transport structures often effectively banning disabled people from using them mirrors a cultural attitude that says it's perfectly acceptable that disabled people cannot even access their own homes. It appears to speak to that classic belief that disabled people – different, special, abnormal – don't have the same needs or subsequent rights as other people.

Like much provision for disability, the crisis of inaccessible homes is a postcode lottery. Some local authorities have taken measures to make improvements for disabled residents. In the capital, the London Plan stipulates that the majority of new homes are built to Lifetime Homes standard (the sixteen design criteria intended to make homes more easily adaptable for lifetime use), while Brighton and Hove set requirements to build some accessible homes on large developments only. Talk to a housing officer and the impression is that developers are reluctant to build accessible houses, as they see them as less profitable, and yet most councils do little about it: according to the EHRC, only 3 per cent have taken action against developers for not complying with accessibility regulations.[6]

In 2018, private housebuilders were caught lobbying councils against building accessible homes for disabled people, in effect actively sabotaging attempts across England to fix new targets to increase accessible housing.[7] The Home Builders Federation (HBF), which represents housing firms, including Persimmon, which recorded gross profits of over £560 million in the first six months of 2018, argued that new local planning policies seeking more accessible housing could make it 'unprofitable to build new homes'.[8] Building to a higher accessibility standard, disability organizations note, would cost as little as £500 more.[9]

The lack of accessible housing is compounded by the fact it is increasingly difficult to obtain the funding to adapt existing inaccessible homes. Local authorities are responsible for providing disabled facilities grants (DFGs) to help disabled people meet the cost of adapting a property, up to a maximum of £30,000 – say, a ramp to get a wheelchair over the step at the front door or installing a stairlift to help them get up to bed. But charities report that these grants are increasingly hard to get from cash-strapped councils, while others are creating near endless delays. There are time limits for how long a disabled person should wait for help in an inaccessible home (current rules mean no disabled person should wait longer than eighteen months to get a decision on a DFG), but by 2015, Leonard Cheshire found at least two-thirds of councils were breaking the law.[10] One charity told me of a family who had to wait so long for their council to agree to adapt their home for their disabled daughter that she died while waiting.

Over the coming years, this crisis is only set to increase. It's estimated by the EHRC that demand for wheelchair-accessible homes will rise by 80 per cent by 2023.[11] Increasing the supply of homes, and reviewing how disabled people are treated in the housing system, while gathering – and making available to potential tenants – information about the availability of accessible housing in their local area could all go some way to meet this need, and to enable people with disabilities to secure a home. And yet there is no national planning policy that specifically considers accessible and adaptable housing for disabled people, and as such local authorities have no obligation to make sure they're delivering the right kind of housing.

Even as politicians make some moves to begin to address Britain's housing crisis, disabled people will continue to be ignored. When the government released the social housing Green Paper in 2018 – described by Communities Secretary

James Brokenshire as a 'new deal' for social housing residents – there wasn't a single mention of accessible housing.[12] (It referred to funding to make disabled people's homes more accessible, and supportive housing for people with learning disabilities and mental health problems.) This erasure of disabled people can be found in all major plans for house building. The Scottish government, for example, will build 50,000 homes by 2021 but, like most local authorities across Britain, there's no target to ensure a proportion are fit for wheelchair access. Worse still, the average council has little grasp of the scale of the problem. An EHRC inquiry found that only 22 per cent of English councils have an accessible-housing register, meaning that politicians aren't monitoring provision and disabled people have nowhere to turn in their search for accessible homes.[13]

To leave millions of people to fester in inaccessible housing in the years to come is inhumane, but it is also incompetent short-termism. Create a housing market that provides disabled people with a home suitable to their needs and we can be healthier, more independent and engaged in work and community. Withhold it and our ability to contribute to society plummets, while social care bills go up, and the NHS takes the cost of avoidable accidents. Leonard Cheshire calculates that the financial cost of inaccessible homes to the NHS and care services is as much as £450 million a year, with 15,000 hours of GP appointments being taken up in the space of a month by people injured through living in unsuitable homes.[14]

Being without a suitable home inevitably has a negative effect on anyone's life — whether that's not being able to reach life goals such as having children or the insecurity of finding employment without a permanent address. But for disabled people, this impact can be profound. Research by Mind in 2018 found that nearly 80 per cent of people with mental health problems say a housing situation has caused a mental health problem or made their mental health worse.[15]

This research didn't take into account the relationship between physical and mental health but it is not a stretch to consider how debilitating living like this can be on mental well-being. Urinate daily in a bottle because you can't get your wheelchair in the bathroom and it's easy to feel you're losing your dignity. Find yourself housebound because you can't get out of your flat and a job becomes impossible: the 2016 LSE report found that disabled people living in inaccessible homes are four times more likely to be unemployed.[16] Even those without existing anxiety or depression are inevitably made more psychologically vulnerable by a housing crisis. 'I no longer feel human,' Robert notes on the impact on him of being trapped in his flat. 'I feel like I no longer have permission to be part of society . . . That I'm excluded from any form of dignity or human rights . . . to be dragged around and caged.'

As councils are cut to the bone, housing shortages are inextricably linked to the social care crisis. In short, poor housing only increases the need for carer workers. Like many disabled people stuck in inaccessible housing, Robert is also living with a shrunken social care package. Despite his medical team explaining he needs 24/7 support, social care cuts mean Robert is left alone for large parts of the day; the equivalent of over four days a week. Without his wheelchair in the flat, he's unable to move, and with no personal assistant, he can't reach a drink or even change his incontinence pads. 'I sit in the same position or I fall on the floor in my own mess,' he says.

Being left to live like this for years has not only taken its toll on Robert's mental health, it is also helping to destroy his body. In 2017 he was turned down for an NHS rehabilitation programme on the grounds of his housing situation. The programme might have helped him keep some movement in his torso but he was told that while he lives in his current flat – and his body is taking the strain of being dragged around – his living conditions would undo any progress he made. A year later, his health had deteriorated to such a degree that he had almost fully lost his voice due to paralysis. In our last conversations, we had to communicate by email. Having to be physically dragged downstairs has caused irreparable damage to Robert's health. He writes, 'My medical team are now currently looking at a double below-the-knee amputation.'

Millions of Britons are in insecure, poor-quality homes against a cocktail of fading social housing, lack of affordable new builds and high private rents. A 2018 report from the Resolution Foundation predicted that one in three millennials will never own their own home; half will be renting in their forties, with a third even likely to be doing so as they claim their pensions.[17] While intergenerational inequality is a defining feature of the modern era, the push to private renting that's characterized housing in recent years goes far beyond the young: a record 1.13 million people aged fifty and over were renting from private landlords in 2018, compared with 651,000 a decade earlier.[18] In a land of shrinking social housing stock and rocketing house prices, the private landlord is increasingly king. In 2018, research by the Housing and Finance Institute showed that 6 million more people are living in short-term rented housing than fifteen years ago as a result of the explosion in private renting, with fewer and fewer Britons owning their own homes or living in social housing.[19]

Such a reliance on the private sector is a worry – many families struggle to afford rising rents yet lack the rights that come with homeownership – but it's a state of affairs that's particularly damaging to disabled people. The vast majority of private rented contracts are assured shorthold tenancies and, as it stands, any landlord can evict a tenant with just two months' notice after a fixed-term period under a Section 21 agreement without providing any reason at all. That's grim for anybody, but if you're a disabled person on a low wage or benefits, having to find the money to move, to pay fees and for a deposit can be impossible. As a result, disabled tenants risk homelessness if they can't find new suitable accommodation.

Many private landlords outright refuse to take tenants if they pay their rent with social security; a form of discrimination that's akin to putting a 'No Disabled, No Poor' sign in the window. People who receive disability benefits are three times more likely to need a housing benefit top-up. Research by Shelter and the National Housing Federation (NHF) in 2018 found that discrimination by letting agents against housing benefit tenants is rife, with disabled people and women the most affected.[20] This discrimination is only increasing. In 2017, the National Landlords Association (NLA) found that only 18–20 per cent of private landlords accepted tenants who pay their rent with the housing benefit, local housing allowance (LHA), down from 46 per cent in 2010–11, while it's feared that this will only worsen further with the roll-out of Universal Credit by 2023 as landlords become wary of the huge rise in non-payment of rent in areas where UC was first introduced.[21]

Meanwhile, a private rental property is often the least accessible option. Housing built for private rent is generally at a lower accessibility standard than other properties, while even gaining information on whether a property is suitable for someone's disability is a struggle. Estate agents, for example, do not typically provide information about the accessibility of private lets (or houses for sale). In addition, with no little irony, many estate agents' premises, small and up a few steps, are inaccessible themselves to disabled people who can't even physically get into the place.

To make matters worse, private sector landlords are notoriously reluctant to permit even small-scale adaptations to make a home more accessible. As one young renter who needed grab rails fitted into his bathroom told me, 'My landlord won't even let us put picture frames up.'

This is far from a niche problem. As well as the flood of young disabled renters wanting to move out of their family homes, research by the National Housing Federation in 2018 into the 'baby boomers' housing crisis' found that nearly three-quarters of older renters have a disability or chronic illness. Many were subsequently struggling with insecure contracts and unsuitable homes. Of people who need vital changes to be made to their homes, such as adding handrails, ramps or wider doorways for their wheelchair, around one in six reported not being able to wash themselves independently as a result of not being allowed adaptations, while two-fifths have had a fall.[22]

Social housing, in principle, should be a solution to this. Disabled people are more likely to live in social housing, as it's more affordable, it tends to provide more security of tenure, and landlords are more willing to install adaptations and provide support, if required. But diminishing housing stock following the right-to-buy policy of the 1980s and a failure by successive governments to invest in new builds means that a chronic shortage is shutting off this option. The number of new, government-funded social homes has fallen by ninety-seven per year since 2010, with just 1,102 new homes completed in 2017.[23]

Need outstrips supply by staggering proportions in many boroughs around the country. A major cross-party commission into social housing in 2019 concluded that more than 3 million new social homes would be needed by 2040 to cope with demand – equating to the biggest social house building drive in England's history, including the two decades after the end of the Second World War.[24] As things stand, research by housing charity Shelter in 2018 found that over a million people across the country are waiting years for a home. Almost two-thirds are on lists for more than twelve months. Meanwhile more than a quarter can wait for more than five years.[25] Some, particularly the poorest, are left waiting their entire adult lives. The BBC documentary *No Place to Call Home* in 2016 found that the deprived London council Barking and Dagenham had fifty times more people on the housing waiting list than properties available.[26] The waiting time for a home was up to fifty years.

In theory, disabled people are relatively protected from such a crisis, as some will be eligible for a higher-needs band aimed at getting them a property more quickly. In reality, many disabled people are deemed ineligible by their council for priority bidding, while the deficit in accessible properties means that there are substantially fewer properties for them to bid on. Giving a wheelchair user first dibs on a tower bloc flat with no lift is less a help and more a cruel tease.

The impact of this is that disabled people are increasingly pushed into the private rental market, and, by extension, into severe financial hardship. A report in 2018 by the charity the Nationwide Foundation found that one million 'vulnerable people' on low incomes, including families with a disabled member, are being driven into deeper poverty due to the acute shortage of social housing as they are forced to pay above the odds for unsuitable private rentals.[27] It pointed to the changes to the benefit system – including benefit sanctions and the roll-out of universal credit – having 'created vulnerability', with families including a disabled person on low incomes in a significantly more precarious position in trying to avoid mounting arrears and eviction than was the case ten years ago.

Disabled people, then, are increasingly caught in a vicious circle of housing: where the drop in affordable and social housing, mixed with a nationwide shortage of accessible properties, shuts us out of finding a suitable home. Meanwhile the rise of short-term private rental contracts, combined with growing economic pressures on both local councils and families, blocks us from adapting an inaccessible property. There is a growing by-product of this broken system: being dumped in temporary accommodation – poor-quality bed-and-breakfast accommodation, private hostels or short-stay shared houses.

Fuchsia has been living out of a budget hotel for four

months. The thirty-three-year-old uses a wheelchair; a spinal injury and displaced hips mean swollen joints and spikes of pain, while fibromyalgia leads to bouts of exhausting fatigue. It was the end of 2017 when she first became homeless after her temporary flat – staying in a friend's spare room – fell through. A more permanent home had evaded her: she couldn't find a flat that was accessible for her wheelchair in Bournemouth, and when she did, private landlords would not rent to her because she was on benefits. Unable to stay with her friend any longer, Fuchsia slept in her car.

The strain on her body after only a few nights led her to be admitted to hospital, where an NHS homeless worker offered to take her to her local council for help. After a five-hour wait, she was told they'd found her somewhere to stay: a hotel room in Crawley, West Sussex, miles away from her primary care team and support network. Living out of a hotel is difficult for anyone, but for someone with a disability or health condition, it can be particularly gruelling. Stuck in an unfamiliar area and without a permanent address, Fuchsia couldn't get a GP to help with her pain meds or her catheter. 'I was so, so ill,' she says. For two weeks, she bounced between the hospital and hotel while becoming increasingly distressed and in pain. By the end of the fortnight, Fuchsia attempted suicide. She survived, but the strain of the accommodation had taken its toll on her mentally and physically. 'My health was rock bottom,' she says.

More than 280,000 people were living in temporary accommodation in Britain as of 2017 – equivalent to around one in every 210 – according to figures obtained by Shelter.[28] (A further 21,300 were in single homeless hostels or social services housing, while 4,500 were sleeping rough.[29]) Such a number is an underestimate, the charity noted, as they did not include people trapped in so-called 'hidden homelessness', who have nowhere to live but are not recorded as needing housing assistance. The National Audit Office calculates that the number of households in temporary accommodation increased by 60 per cent between 2011 and 2017.[30] The dramatic rise in temporary accommodation has characterized the senselessness of the housing crisis in recent years: instead of building more homes, ministers shell out hundreds of millions[31] to private landlords cramming people into short-term lets. For disabled people like Fuchsia, it's little more than a holding pen: with no accessible properties available for them, they are bounced around B&Bs, budget chain hotels, and short-stay properties as they wait for months or even years for the council to find them a suitable home. In this climate, a Premier Inn is Britain's new social housing.

With her health worsening, Fuchsia's council moved her to another hotel, this time in Newhaven across the county in East Sussex. It was better-quality – her bed had a specialist mattress suitable for her disability – but at £170 a night, within a week the council had moved her again, now to a cheaper lodge in Eastbourne. As she puts it to me, 'I went from being on an orthopaedic bed and a clean room to being in hell.'

The bed was so high that Fuchsia often could not transfer safely onto it from a chair. When she was strong enough to get onto the bed, the mattress sent her back muscles into spasms; the only way she can sleep is on top of two pillows and a quilt. The bathroom wasn't cleaned regularly so Fuchsia kept slipping on the wet floor. The first time I speak to Fuchsia, she is in hospital after falling over in the bathroom when staff had not mopped it. 'Everything went from beneath me . . . I hit the floor like a sack of potatoes,' she explained on the phone.

Living out of a hotel means there are no kitchen facilities so Fuchsia cannot make herself a meal. Instead, she lives from a mini fridge; big enough to fit in yogurt and cheese but not much else. To have a hot meal, she has to pay for takeaway – spending ten pounds a day out of her benefits – or, if not, she eats cup-a-soups or noodles. A friend has just bought her a rice cooker 'so at least I have one hot meal a day', and she's mainly living off crackers, pesto and cold Heinz soup. It's taking its toll on her health: she's developed malnutrition and anaemia and is visibly pale with grey circles under her eyes. Hunger is hard enough when you're healthy, but when you're already fatigued or weak it's like an assault on the body. When Fuchsia's in hospital, the nurses get her to eat two hot meals before she goes back to the hotel, she says. 'I've got enough problems without not eating properly. But I've got no choice.'

Such conditions are reflective of a wider picture of how those on waiting lists are forced to live. Research by the Institute for Public Policy Research in 2016 found temporary accommodation in Britain to be plagued by squalid, damp and dangerous conditions, with tenants reporting kitchens infested with cockroaches, quilts soaked in blood, and no heating.[32] One tenant was forced to sleep in their coat and scarf in order not to touch or 'breathe in disease'. It's a dark irony: the very people trying to gain stability are often put in accommodation that makes their life worse. Vulnerable people sent to homes with abusive management and tenants. Those with breathing problems expected to live in properties that have environmental health warnings. Individuals who already have weakened bodies now unable to make regular meals or wash without adequate kitchen and bathroom facilities. Or wheelchair users shoved in high-rise buildings with inadequate fire safety.

Fuchsia is not even able to use her wheelchair at her current hotel. There is no disabled parking outside, which means she can't safely get her chair out of her car; instead, she has to park on the seafront on a thirty-mile-an-hour road ('I tried twice to get my wheelchair out and two cars nearly hit me,' she explains). Besides, the ramp going into the hotel is too steep for a wheelchair and there's no automatic door; once, she tells me, she fell out of her wheelchair trying to get through the door, tipping back and hitting the floor. After that, she left her wheelchair in the car and started using her walking sticks to get inside. Unable to have the safety of using her wheelchair in the hotel, she's now regularly having falls. 'I've had to call the ambulance service four times in a month because of this,' she says.

Even without accidents, Fuchsia is normally reliant on heavy-duty pain meds but because she's in temporary accommodation, she has no way to access them. She's now out of her medication but because she can't register as a full patient at a GP surgery until she has a permanent address, no one will prescribe them to her. Instead, she's falling back on increasingly desperate measures. She's turning to A & E for morphine; she'll go to the emergency ward, come back to the hotel, and then repeat. On one occasion she had to remove her own catheter at the hotel because she couldn't get a community nurse to come and see her. Out of borough and cut off from support networks, she's also a forty-five-minute drive from her nearest friend. There is no phone signal in the hotel, so in case of a health emergency, she has to somehow get herself outside on her crutches if she needs to contact someone, even the paramedics.

Months of living like this mean, in Fuchsia's words, she's 'losing it'. 'I have begged and begged for help,' she says. 'I'm struggling to continue any more. I am so, so sick.' The council offered her a property at one point but it was so inaccessible that she couldn't get her wheelchair in and out of it. Turning properties down always comes with danger: people who refuse to take what the council offers risk being found 'intentionally homeless' under homelessness legislation, meaning there is then no further legal duty for a council to help them.

Fuchsia knows there's an added risk for disabled people like her: if the council repeatedly offer her inaccessible housing, she could find herself kicked off the housing list entirely, simply for turning down properties she cannot physically get in. On top of this, there's a fear that disabled people will be turned away by councils for being 'too much trouble'. In December 2016, a piece by the campaign group Sisters Uncut for the *Guardian* reported that homeless people with learning difficulties, for example, are more likely to be turned away as local authorities feel they don't have the resources to provide the appropriate care.[33]

Months later, Fuchsia contacted me to say she had been moved into another temporary accommodation – this time a two-bed ground-floor flat. It is a reprieve – she is out of the hotels and is no longer classed as being in emergency housing. But it is still partly inaccessible. The bathroom is so tiny she can't fit her wheelchair near the sink, ('You can sit on the edge of the bath and wash your face in the sink. That's how small it is,' she says), which means she can't use the toilet. Instead, Fuchsia is forced to have a commode; a plastic seat and a potty for a bathroom. Because it's temporary accommodation, she's also not allowed to make even minor adaptations to the property: grab rails in the bathroom or an electric motor on the front door to help her get in. Outside her area, it's still miles away from her support network. She has a roof over her head, but it's not quite a home.

At a time of a shortage of social housing, falling homeownership and rising private rents, housing benefit – the means-tested rent support paid to around 5 million low-income tenants – is a lifeline for many. But just as families were finding it harder to keep a roof over their heads, austerity policies were introduced that withdrew the housing benefit they needed to pay the rent.

From the coalition government to Theresa May's administration, recent years have seen a range of policies brought in that have decimated the housing safety net. The local housing allowance (LHA), introduced in 2008 by the last Labour government to bring the amount being spent on housing benefit for those renting privately in line with the benefit for those renting social housing, was severely tightened under David Cameron, often leading to less housing benefit being paid for the same accommodation. That this was done at a time of increased private rents meant there was often now no link between LHA and what was actually needed to pay the rent, pushing low-income families into mounting arrears.

Meanwhile, the benefit cap, a policy that put a limit on how much a household could receive in social security, made it even harder to pay the rent. First introduced in 2013, the benefit cap epitomized the narrative of the benefit shirker versus the hardworking taxpayer perpetuated by the coalition, harking back to the idea that hordes of benefit claimants were enjoying an easy life compared to workers. As then chancellor George Osborne said in 2012, 'Where is the fairness, we ask, for the shift-worker, leaving home in the dark hours of the early morning, who looks up at the closed blinds of their next-door neighbour sleeping off a life on benefits.'[34]

The policy was so popular that the government lowered the cap even further in 2016. In doing so, it saw 10,000 additional disabled people have their benefits reduced, often by more than £100 or even £150 a week.[35] The Department for Work and Pension's own research showed that ministers were fully aware that disabled people would be disproportionately hit: 'of the households who lose from this policy . . . we expect roughly half will contain somebody who is classed as disabled under the Equality Act,' it read.[36] Because of their disability, these were often people who had no way of moving into work in order to escape the cap. The infamous neighbour 'sleeping off a life of benefits' was in fact too sick to get out of bed in the morning.

But it was the bedroom tax that in many ways came to symbolize the worst of such changes; a policy that led to as many as 660,000 people in social housing have their housing benefit docked for having a so-called 'spare' room, which saw families lose an average of £728 each year.[37] The bedroom tax uniquely targeted disabled people, with almost half of all those affected having a disability.[38] Like other so-called welfare reforms, from the offset, a policy that was set to cause incredible harm to disabled people was presented as some sort of moral mission. 'It's unfair to subsidise spare rooms in the social sector if you don't subsidise them in the private sector,' David Cameron said in the House of Commons in 2016. 'That is a basic issue of fairness.'[39]

Look at right-wing newspaper headlines or listen to a government 'welfare' minister debate the bedroom tax and the impression is of a disabled person milking the taxpayer to enjoy a spacious guest room. In reality, these were box rooms lined with adult nappies and oxygen cylinders. Many of the 'spare rooms' that disabled people had their benefits docked for were in fact being used to store vital medical equipment or for a carer to sleep in. Regardless, the public widely supported it: an opinion poll on the bedroom tax by Ipsos Mori in 2013 found that only a quarter of people were against the policy.[40]

The result was wheelchair users skipping meals. In 2013, only a few months after the policy was brought in, research by the charity Papworth Trust found that nine in ten disabled people were being forced to cut back on food or paying household bills after being refused emergency housing payments to help them pay the bedroom tax.[41] At the same time, Carers UK found that one in six carers interviewed over the first 100 days of the bedroom tax reported that they were facing eviction after falling behind on the rent.[42] That's families caring for loved ones with cancer, or looking after a severely disabled child. It was only after a legal challenge in 2017 that the government was forced to exempt carers from the bedroom tax.[43]

I asked a manager of a London-based mental health

charity if many disabled people came through the service after experiencing homelessness. 'A lot of people I know have lost their homes due to the bedroom tax,' she said. 'Many are now sleeping on other people's sofas, or in hostels. Others are pet-sitting in other peoples homes, some live in tents, some do DIY work round the country to get a home.'

Even the apparent motivation for the policy – that it would 'encourage' social tenants to downsize to smaller properties – penalized disabled people. Freedom of Information requests by the Labour Party in 2013 found that 96 per cent of those affected had, in effect, nowhere to move to; the deficit in one-bed properties in the social housing stock meant that they were trapped in their larger homes even if they wanted to downsize to avoid the tax.[44]

Worse, many disabled tenants' homes are heavily adapted properties; wet rooms, grab rails and ramps fitted by their council over the years to help them live independently. It means that the bedroom tax – supposedly another step in bringing the 'welfare' bill down – was in effect forcing disabled people to leave behind expensive renovations only to move to a smaller property that would then need adapting all over again. It was another rigged game: in a climate in which it was harder than ever to hold on to your home, the bedroom tax docked disabled people's housing benefit while knowing that they had little to no way of escaping it.

Precariousness has in many ways come to define the housing crisis, in which more and more families teeter on the brink of eviction due to a cocktail of rising private rents, squeezed wages and benefit cuts. Homelessness – from living in temporary and emergency accommodation to sleeping rough – is the inevitable consequence. In addition to the rise in temporary accommodation, street sleeping has subsequently similarly rocketed in recent years. Going about their day in the years after the recession, no one could fail to notice the renewed presence of rough sleepers: a tent pitched in the local park, rows of sleeping bags on the pavement, makeshift communities of rubbish and blankets housed in the underpass.

More than 12,000 people in Britain are now sleeping rough, according to a report by the charity Crisis in 2018, with a further 12,000 spending their nights in tents, cars, sheds, night buses or even bins.[45] The National Audit Office (NAO) estimates rough sleeping has increased by 134 per cent since 2010, with the number of people living on the streets increasing every year since the coalition government first took power.[46] Ministers have been quick to pass the buck, with the housing secretary, James Brokenshire, declaring in December 2018 that growing homelessness was down to drug use and family breakdown rather than government policy (he was later forced to partly climb-down from his comments).[47] The evidence, however, says something quite different. An independent study in 2015 by the Homelessness Monitor, published by Crisis and the Joseph Rowntree Foundation, found 'welfare reforms' to be 'fuelling' this rapidly worsening homelessness.[48] It said that policies including the bedroom tax, sanctions and housing benefit cuts were the biggest single trigger for homelessness after the economy had recovered from the 2008 global crash, with households in London found to be particularly vulnerable.

If you wanted a symbol of the retreat of the state, few

would be stronger than the sight of more people sleeping rough. In the age of austerity, homelessness is no longer simply a reality for those on the edge of society, the sad result of a chaotic life or drug and alcohol addiction. Increasingly, almost anyone could find themselves at risk of losing their home; all it takes is the loss of a job, a benefit delay, an insecure tenancy or a spell of ill health. The very people who were previously said to be cushioned from the threat of homelessness find themselves being pushed further to the brink of losing their homes. In 2017 the local government ombudsman warned that even working families were increasingly finding themselves with nowhere to live after losing their private tenancy.[49] With emergency accommodation stretching council services, it was suddenly not beyond possibility that rough sleeping might become someone's only option.

This precariousness was only furthered by the fact that cuts to local authorities targeted services that in the past had helped nip problems in the bud before a crisis turned into homelessness, from mental health services, debt advice and welfare rights advisers to relationship mediation services. Similarly, outreach services that previously assisted rough sleepers to take the difficult steps back into housing and employment increasingly turned threadbare or had to shut their doors entirely.

Research by homelessness charity St Mungo's in 2016 identified lack of specialist mental health provision as the main cause of increased rough sleeping: four out of ten people whom homelessness workers came into contact with had at least one mental health problem, yet 86 per cent reported a lack of beds for people with mental health issues.[50]

The report calculated that, on average, local authority funding for services for helping 'vulnerable people' avoid homelessness was cut by 45 per cent in the five years from when David Cameron's coalition took power.[51] Not only had austerity cuts increased the odds of someone becoming homeless; they had also shredded the safety net that might previously have caught them.

What's precarious for healthy renters is particularly so for disabled people – who are less likely to be in work or have a high wage and are typically more reliant on social security, while having less choice in the private rental market and higher odds of being cut off from social housing due to the lack of accessible properties. This translated into an explosion in the number of disabled people without a home since the recession. Figures from the Department for Communities and Local Government in December 2017 showed that disabled people have been disproportionately hit by increasing homelessness, with homelessness (defined as including those in temporary accommodation as well as rough sleepers) among people with mental and physical health problems having increased by around 75 per cent since 2010.

Paul has ME and has been sleeping rough in London for nine years. For a decade, the fifty-year-old was working in public relations in the capital, earning £40,000 at his highest point. But holding down a job with a debilitating illness was an uphill battle – 'By the time I left the company I literally couldn't string two words together,' he says of his last role – and in 2001 he had to stop altogether. As for many, the trigger of Paul's homelessness was losing his private tenancy; an error with a credit rating was enough for him to be evicted from his flat. The stress brought on an ME relapse – exhaustion so severe that he couldn't get out of bed and was hospitalized for three months. For a while, he was a 'bed blocker' – technically well enough to leave but with nowhere else to go, he fought to keep his bed. 'I wouldn't let them discharge me to the streets in a wheelchair,' he says. 'They did that to some poor unfortunate a few weeks after me and he died the next day.'

To die on Britain's streets is not a rarity. The Bureau of Investigative Journalism (BIJ) in 2018 found that more than 440 homeless people had died unhoused or in temporary accommodation in the UK in the past year.[52] A former soldier, an astrophysicist and a *Big Issue* seller were among the hundreds found dead in shop doorways, hostels and camping in tents in woodland. Some lay dead for months before their bodies were discovered. Due to the nature of homelessness, studies into deaths vary in their calculations, but each consistently shows a surge in deaths since austerity policies first kicked in. Figures compiled by the *Guardian* in 2018 found the number of homeless people recorded dying on the streets or in temporary accommodation in the UK had more than doubled over the last five years, with the number increasing year on year since 2013.[53] In the capital, where Paul rough sleeps and the only place where a local authority actively records homeless deaths, on average one homeless person died every fortnight between 2010 and 2017.[54]

It is not hard to imagine how brutal conditions, from sub-zero temperatures, to violence, to a lack of food or medication, leave people with existing physical illness or mental health problems particularly vulnerable to losing their life, especially at a time when specialist services are dwindling. Deaths of rough sleepers with mental health problems, for example, have subsequently risen sharply in recent years, with the St Mungo's research showing that four out of five rough sleepers who died in London in 2017 had mental health needs, an increase from three in ten in 2010.[55] In March 2019, the *Daily Mirror* reported the harrowing case of a disabled woman who died on the streets of Leeds in her wheelchair. Known as Tasher by friends and thought to be in her fifties, her body was found in the doorway of House of Fraser.[56] There are large swathes of others, like Tasher, at risk: research by disability homelessness charity Good4you estimates that as much as half of London's homeless population is disabled, be it with physical or mental health problems.[57]

While ministers speak of promises to always protect 'the most vulnerable', it is the people who are struggling with mental illness, fatigue or pain who are in many ways most likely to become homeless. Research from Groundswell, a charity working to support homeless people, in 2018 found that over half of homeless people suffer from chronic pain conditions, such as arthritis (that's compared to only 12.5 per cent among the general population).[58] The charity highlighted that this was a vicious cycle: while the conditions that come with homelessness can lead to chronic pain, almost four in ten of respondents said that pain had contributed to their becoming homeless. Among these participants, nearly seven in ten said that pain made it difficult for them to hold down a job, while half said that pain had caused trouble in personal relationships.[59]

In the end, Paul was discharged from hospital to a hostel

in Brixton; largely bedbound and only able to move with a wheelchair. His local council gave him two options: go on the list for accessible social housing – with an approximately seven-year waiting time – or sign up with a private lettings agency that specialized in helping to house people on benefits. He took the second option. 'A bad move,' he says, in retrospect. By doing so, it meant that the council rescinded their obligation to find him alternative accommodation.

Instead, for two years, Paul slept out of his car – a Mini – with his wheelchair folded down in the back and Paul squashed on the passenger seat. Hellish for anyone, but when you're disabled, it's torture. Stress and physical exertion are common triggers for an ME relapse and homelessness is a breeding ground. The Groundswell research found that as many as almost nine in ten homeless people (including those with no pre-existing health problems) felt that sleeping rough had an impact on their physical health: from the aches and pains of sleeping out, or the back pain from carrying a backpack all day, to the pain caused to feet from walking around between services.[60] Once, Paul was stuck in his car for three days straight during a relapse, unable to move or even talk. 'That was incredibly frightening,' he admits.

In the end, the police confiscated the car and Paul had to go back to his council for help. Housing officers asked for proof he was homeless but because he had insurance for his car under his old address, they took it as 'proof' that he had a home and refused to help. This refusal is far from uncommon. In 2014, homeless charity Crisis sent 'mystery shoppers' (actors posing as single homeless people) to sixteen local authorities across the country in a bid to monitor the service being provided.[61] On a number of occasions, mystery shoppers – some of whom played very vulnerable characters – were denied any type of help until they could prove that they were homeless and eligible for assistance, while the local authorities in question made no effort to make enquiries themselves or provide temporary accommodation in the interim. This was particularly the case in London, where housing pressures are especially significant.

Eventually, the council offered Paul some emergency accommodation – what they claimed to be wheelchair-accessible. In fact, it was a third-floor room in a block with no lift; there were four more steps to get up at the front door, and a doorway so narrow that he couldn't get inside in his wheelchair. When Paul viewed it, the door had been kicked in. There were bloodstains on the mattress. 'I couldn't even sit down,' he says of the dirt. With no help from his council, Paul started what turned into years of bouncing between makeshift beds. Sofa-surfing in friends' homes, or borrowing their cars to sleep in. Hostels. Night shelters. 'Most have wheelchair access,' he says. Desperation started to mix with innovation. He slept for three months in a terminal at Heathrow airport. Even a disabled toilet for a while. As he puts it, 'Simply anything to survive.'

Wherever he goes, Paul carries with him his remaining possessions: a cracked iPad and a large Louis Vuitton bag containing some clothes and toiletries. They are as much practical help as signs of better times; his Louis Vuitton bag was purchased with his first ever decent pay cheque when he was headhunted, he recalls. 'It's been my hold-all ever since and has been my one saving grace being homeless,' he explains. 'When police spot me sleeping at Heathrow airport, they think I'm travelling and leave me alone.'

After Paul lost his car, he lost the place to store his wheel-chair; nowadays, it sits in a storage unit in Battersea. It means that if he has a fatigue crash when he's not using it, he's stuck wherever he is at the time – unable to walk but unable to access his wheelchair either. 'But the security of knowing it's there if I needed it . . . that I could send a friend to pick it up . . . does bring some comfort,' he says. In the spring of 2018, he had an ME relapse so severe that he couldn't speak, let alone walk. Being bedbound is particularly brutal when you don't have your own bed, and for four months he slept in a friend's spare bedroom, unable to move and waiting to be well enough to get his wheelchair back.

Throughout it all, Disability Living Allowance (DLA) has been Paul's only way to buy food, toiletries or a night in a shelter. But in the middle of his relapse, as welfare 'reform' kicked in, Paul was summoned to an assessment centre to test if he should keep his disability benefit. He had no way to get to the appointment: the test centre he'd been allocated was thirty miles away from where he usually sleeps rough and he has no home to do a home visit in. This isn't the first time he's been in this situation; over the years, he's applied for benefits and appealed decisions almost twenty times. More exhaustion, just to be able to eat. He tends to use a friend's home for assessments, but this time round officials refused. In the end, he was turned down for his benefits. The assessors said he failed to turn up to the appointment. 'Even knowing I was bedridden,' he says.

Over the years, rather than being a safety net, social secu-rity has helped keep Paul on the streets. He's had ongoing errors with his housing benefit being incorrectly stopped, resulting in his repeatedly being evicted from shelters when he has no way to pay. Both of his disability benefits have been removed, in part because of his homelessness; officials refused to send him appointment notifications in an email, even though he has no address for them to post letters to. As he moved out of his friend's flat, after eighteen months waiting, Paul got a backdated disability benefit payment of £2,000 with more to come – enough to pay friends back money he'd borrowed over the years to survive. Because he has no bank account, he has to use the 'voucher' system to get any benefits; in short, he's emailed a voucher and has to cash it in at a Paypoint store. Budgeting or making plans with this system is next to impossible. 'The vouchers come in spurious amounts . . . and don't tell you what benefit they relate to, for what period, or total amount,' he explains.

In the coming years, the risk of homelessness in Britain is only set to increase. In 2018, the government launched the Homeless Reduction Act, which required local authorities to actively take steps to prevent people at risk of homelessness tipping into crisis. But this will do little without sufficient funding for local government, particularly at a time of pressure caused by housing shortages, rising rents and benefit cuts. If current policies continue unchanged, Crisis estimates that the number of households in temporary accommodation is set to nearly double over the next decade, with rough sleeping projected to rise by over 75 per cent.[62]

Disabled people, as ever, are at greatest risk. Shelter says that more than 200,000 households that include a disabled person are in danger of becoming homeless by 2020 because of rising rents, benefit freezes and a lack of social housing.[63] While policies such as the bedroom tax continue, Universal Credit, set to roll out to as many as 8 million families by

2023, will likely push tenants further towards eviction. A report by the NAO, the public spending watchdog, in 2018 found that widespread errors mean a quarter of claims are paid late,[64] so people's debts and rent arrears soar, while the mental health charity, Mind, warned that 750,000 disabled people could be left 'penniless' in the transfer to the new system.[65]

In London, I speak to Paul again from a friend's house; he's using their washing machine to wash his one set of spare clothes and borrow some more. He's desperate: the week earlier he had his precious Louis Vuitton bag taken as he slept on a bus, and with it, his daily clothes, soap and deodorant. 'I had my life stolen,' he says. He's grateful he's not currently bedbound from his ME – he's 'functioning' about three or four days out of the week, he says – but is constantly exhausted and looking for a way to rest. If he can get his housing benefit sorted, he hopes to go back to the council to ask again for them to house him. In the meantime, he's clinging to any upside. 'I'm still alive,' he says.

CHAPTER 5

Women

For the last five years, Alice, twenty-four, has been making a living as a sex worker. She's also disabled; she has bipolar type II that leads to mania, depression and severe lack of physical energy.

For Alice, the two sides of her life – her disability and sex work – are inexorably linked. Alice (not her real name) started this line of work when she was nineteen and in her second year at university – a way to make some extra cash to top up her student loan. She had always intended to quit sex work after graduating. 'That was three years ago,' she says.

Upon leaving university, she struggled to retain a job. Traditional employment – with a boss and set working hours – proved impossible during manic episodes and her job as a university administrator came to an end for that reason. She started a PGCE in the East Midlands in September 2017 with the hopes of becoming a teacher but her mental health meant she kept missing lectures and the university eventually recommended she take a year out. 'I've to all intents and purposes [had to] drop out,' she says.

The disability benefit system is supposed to be there to catch people like Alice; a safety net for when ill health means she cannot have a job to pay the bills. But she is in a catch-22: she cannot claim the out-of-work sickness benefit, Employment Support Allowance (ESA), because she is still registered as a student, despite the fact that her mental health meant she had to leave her course. 'On the one hand, I've got someone saying, "You're too unwell to study or work." On the other, I've got [the government] saying, "You're not unwell enough to get support, and go away,"' she says.

On top of this, she was turned down for the other key disability benefit, Personal Independence Payment (PIP). In the middle of a manic episode she could not fill in the extensive paperwork. 'Ironically, I wasn't well enough to chase them,' she says. She had to appeal the decision, which constitutes a mound of paperwork and then a tribunal in court. Besides, Alice worries that mental health problems are rarely seen by the benefit system as being as debilitating as, say, being a wheelchair user. It's a concern backed up by evidence: in 2018, the High Court ruled that the PIP system was 'blatantly discriminatory' against people with mental health problems, even going as far as to order the government to review 1.6 million disability benefit claims.[1] It all adds up to a situation where Alice could not pay the bills with either a wage or social security. As she put it to me, 'I've got no income to speak of and the government don't care.'

Instead, she's had to rely on sex work to get by. When I first speak to Alice, she's working. I've accidentally called her early and her client is still in her home. This is an intimate

set up but it generally works for her health. Being in essence
self-employed, she has a flexible working pattern and can
control the use of her own flat. 'When I'm having my down
days, I don't have an employer to answer to, and then when
I'm elated or if I'm actually well, I can sort my own bookings
out and organize my own working pattern to cover the days
that I can't work,' she says.

This is especially easy with sex work, she explains, as she is
able to earn a lot quickly 'if you put the time and energy in'.
However, her mental health means she has often not got
enough energy to take bookings. Alice uses what she calls
'standard rates': £130 for an hour at her place, £150 at someone else's, £50 for fifteen minutes, and £750 for overnight.
Most clients tend to go for half an hour or an hour, she says.
She describes her working hours as 'binge and starve': she
goes several weeks without a client and then sees several men
a day, for a few days. 'Then I recover,' she says.

There is a pressure to take on as many clients as possible when
she is well. Without her disability benefits or a regular income,
Alice is in thousands of pounds of debt: £10,000 to friends she's
borrowed off over the years, her student loan, a £3,000 overdraft, and maxed-out credit cards. Rare periods of hyper-mania
as a result of her bipolar disorder can lead her to shop exces-
sively. But for the last five years, it's simply her lack of income
that has seen her finances spiral. She's getting into more and
more debt every month, as her outgoings exceed her earnings.
The stress of the debts is taking a further toll on her mental
health, 'only making the situation a vicious cycle'. Finding
clients has become a way to alleviate the debt and keep her head
above water. 'I wouldn't have been able to survive without sex
work,' she says. 'It's quite literally saved my life.'

As we talk, Alice repeatedly tells me there are times she really enjoys sex work but she admits her choices are heavily controlled by circumstance. She says, 'I'm definitely being failed by the system right now – being financially coerced into it by the government.'

As the recession and the subsequent austerity measures kicked in, I began to speak to a number of disabled women who had turned to sex work in order to get by. The methods of sex work varied. Some met men in person who paid them in exchange for sex. Others began sex-cam work; half an hour stripping on Skype for a stranger across the Internet. Women with pain- or fatigue-related disabilities were particularly prevalent in the latter. Sex work was the one job they could do from their bed. But if the disabilities varied, the reasons for taking on this work often came back the same: like Alice, without access to benefits or traditional employment, sex work was the only way they could survive.

Alice's best friend Sarah is also a disabled sex worker. She's recovering from surgery for severe endometriosis and has chronic pain, fatigue and ME. Unlike Alice, Sarah (a pseudonym) has been granted disability benefits but does sex work 'under the radar' to 'top up' her low payments. 'They [the government] give her some but not enough. It's not enough to live off as a human being,' Alice says. Many of her friends with disabilities and chronic illnesses started sex work for the ease and flexibility it offered to those who are too unwell for traditional employment – or, as she puts it, whose energy levels are sometimes too low to function properly but 'who need money to survive in the world'. 'It is what it is,' she says. 'If the state won't support vulnerable people, they

have to find work. And if they can't, they'll find options' –
like sex work.

This use of sex work as a last option for marginalized
women is not a new phenomenon, but as benefit cuts were
rolled out, evidence pointed to austerity measures exacerbat-
ing some women's reliance on sex work. As Universal Credit
(UC) came under renewed fire in 2018, Frank Field MP,
chair of the Work and Pensions Committee, reported that
some women in his Birkenhead constituency had been
pushed into prostitution because of the local roll-out of UC,
describing how hardship brought on by the new benefit
system meant that 'some women have taken to the red light
district for the first time'.[2] The union ASLEF suggests that
on-street prostitution increased by 60 per cent between 2010
and 2017, which has in particular been linked to an increase
in women having their benefits sanctioned.[3]

Women's organizations and outreach workers across the
country repeatedly point to this pattern. Changing Lives, a
charity that provides women's services across the North of
England and the Midlands, conducted research in 2016 into
what it termed 'survival sex work'.[4] It found women to be selling penetrative sex for as little as ten pounds for a place to stay
or even in exchange for clean clothes, with 'punters' approach-
ing them to offer as little as a fiver at times when the women
are perceived as being particularly vulnerable. Staff at the
organization's women's outreach centre tell me that a growing
number of women are being pushed into sex work because
they have their benefits stopped for things such as missing
JobCentre appointments or failing to attend interviews.

'We noticed a big increase in women selling sex after the
introduction of benefit sanctions, not just to make ends

meet but, in some cases, to provide the basics for their family,' says Laura Seebohm, director of operations at Changing Lives. 'Some of the women were so desperate that they were selling sex for the first time while others had successfully got themselves out of the world of survival sex only for the sanctions to come along and force them back into it.' Another staff member at the service, Laura McIntyre, told me that women with learning disabilities and those with multiple and complex needs have been particularly at risk of being groomed for the purposes of sexual exploitation. Meanwhile the benefit system contributes in a number of ways to women increasingly relying on sex work. Some have sold sex because they find the benefit system too complex to navigate or cannot keep up with the requirements of the JobCentre in order to access benefits because of their vulnerability. 'Like having to make phone calls,' she says.

At the same time, Sheffield Working Women's Opportunities Project in 2016 warned that austerity measures, including benefit rejections and sanctions, were behind an estimated 400 per cent rise in women using their service who had entered prostitution.[5] While they might normally see between 180 and 195 women in sex work over a whole year, over fifty came through their doors in a three-month period between June and August 2016. 'There are a lot of reasons that women turn to prostitution, but austerity has been one of the biggest factors we've seen in the recent rise,' the manager of the centre told local paper the *Star* in November 2016.[6]

Some were new to sex work, they noted, but many were women who had previously managed to leave prostitution only to have to return as much as a decade later because of losing their social security. This link between benefit payments and sex work was direct. 'We know that some women come out just so they can buy food, and once they've raised enough they go home again,' the manager of the centre went on.[7] 'Quite a lot of women might only intend to come out for five or six weeks to make some money while they wait for payments to come through but once they're in it again, it can be very difficult to leave.'

Alice is, in many ways, in a much safer environment than the women resorting to on-street sex work. She finds her clients through an 'adult webpage' and coordinates them through a work phone and email address. 'Ninety per cent of sex work is admin,' she laughs. But she admits that, even working in this safer environment, she's sometimes more vulnerable because of her mental health. If she's hyper-manic, her mental health doesn't simply lead her to take on more work but to forgo safety checks: during those periods, she's active, creative, energized, 'and everything seems a good idea'. 'It's not necessarily safe. I make riskier decisions – like driving two hours to somewhere I don't know at 3 a.m.,' she says.

At the other end of the spectrum, when depression hits, her energy plummets, sometimes to the extent that she has to cancel clients. It's led to her receiving a couple of negative reviews on 'punt sites' – websites in which men give reviews of sex workers – that she's 'unreliable' because of it. In the end, she tells me, she logged on to explain that, while she was sorry to cancel, she has bipolar and that means that sometimes she doesn't have the energy to spend two hours doing her make-up, shaving and dressing, 'and to pretend to like you'.

It's hard to think how Alice is going to get out of sex work. Her dream is to find a job in teaching – 'I'd like to think [sex work] is not going to be my life,' she says. But it doesn't seem possible to her in the near future. Even getting temporary shop work or admin roles is difficult. On top of the fact that her mental health problems make it hard for her to keep a job or to attend training, gaps on her CV – both from illness spells and long stretches where she's only worked as a sex worker – mean that she knows she's less employable. She sends out multiple CVs and applications every day but is getting nowhere. 'No one will employ me,' she says. 'It's hard to leave this industry. It traps you.'

Alice is doing this at a time when women generally, let alone those contending with health problems, are facing an increasingly arduous labour market. The push to insecure, low-paid work in recent years has disproportionately affected women, who are already more likely than men to be in part-time or low-waged roles. Since the start of the global crash in 2008, 826,000 extra women have moved into low-paid and insecure work, according to the Fawcett Society.[8] At the same time the number of female part-time workers who would like to be working full-time has nearly doubled, to 789,000.[9]

This shift to precarious work will likely exacerbate what are already poorer working opportunities for those women with disabilities. Research by Comic Relief in 2017 found that as much as 50 per cent of the work disabled people perform is in low-paid, short-term and part-time roles, meaning female disabled workers are contending with the impact of both sex and disability.[10] Thanks to the unequal burden of austerity, disabled women, such as Alice, are simultaneously being penalized by both their sex and their disability.

Even cuts to disability benefits are in some ways gendered. Women are more likely to be disabled – there are around 6.4 million disabled women in the UK compared to 5.5 million disabled men – and the Women's Budget Group in 2018 found that almost six in ten individuals claiming Personal Independence Payments are women.[11] When we next talk, Alice has just received a large pack of documents from the DWP: 100 A4 pages front and back. She needs to read and understand all of them before her tribunal appeal of her PIP rejection; a process that has overall taken the best part of a year so far. 'The government is making it deliberately as confusing, intimidating and difficult as possible,' she says. A local disability charity have been helping her navigate the appeal but their Lottery funding – their only source of income – is due to run out in a few months' time and Alice is worried she'll be left to take on officials at the tribunal alone. 'It's all very overwhelming and distressing,' she says. 'I really need the government to recognize that I have next to no income and it is a direct result of being disabled.'

Her mental health is deteriorating as a result. During this period Alice was put under the care of the Crisis Team for suicide prevention after developing suicidal feelings. She came off her meds as they were no longer working. Still, she's sending off multiple CVs each day but, more than ever, she admits, 'I'm not in a place where I can manage a traditional job.' Her health means she's had to go part-time with sex work; she's still taking on clients but she's no longer breaking even from what she earns and it's getting worse every month. She's trying to formally withdraw from her degree so she's eligible for ESA, and with it she might finally get a bit of support from the benefit system. In the meantime, it's a case of borrowing money from friends, credit cards and her growing bank overdraft. 'I don't know what to do at this point,' she admits. 'I'm treading water. Or at least delaying my drowning through . . . sex work.'

When Bethany's husband abused her, 'stupid' was his favourite insult. Bethany, sixty, is Deaf. She first met her husband in London over forty years ago. Back in the early 1980s, he showed no signs of what his future behaviour might be. 'He was lovely,' Bethany says. For the first twenty years of their marriage, they had what she describes as a typical relationship – 'Just normal rows' – but when his mother died, he changed, and the verbal abuse started. *Cunt. Stupid.* 'Every name under the sun,' she says.

I speak to Bethany through a British Sign Language (BSL) interpreter and with the support of Marie, a manager from DeafHope, the UK's only specialist domestic violence service for Deaf women. Bethany's husband never learnt BSL and she could only understand him by lip reading. Soon enough, her disability became part of the abuse. 'He knew I couldn't hear but he'd ask me questions and make out I was stupid,' she says. It became normal for him to exploit the fact she couldn't hear and mock her for it, chipping away at her confidence.

They had two young children – a son and a daughter – and Bethany kept the abuse quiet to try and protect them. With the verbal and psychological abuse came controlling behaviour. 'Everything was about him. He wanted to be in charge. No one could say "no",' she says. 'Everything I did was wrong. Even my best.' Sometimes, she would make dinner only for him to tell her to start again and cook something different. The message was always about him being in control of her: 'I'm your husband so if I say it, you do it.'

Bethany was already isolated due to her disability – she hadn't worked since giving up a cleaning job when she had children and the majority of people around her didn't know sign language. But her husband began to control who she saw and when, eventually stopping her visiting her family. On the rare times that she did visit her parents, her husband would send her a text: 'Come home now.' I ask her what might happen if she didn't go and she shakes her head quickly, gesturing that this was never an option. When she did go back, they argued and the abuse escalated. He physically grabbed her shoulders and shouted in her face, knowing she could feel his screams but not hear his words.

Britain has a pandemic of domestic violence against disabled women, with the charity SafeLives estimating half a million disabled women aged sixteen to sixty-four in the UK are suffering domestic abuse.[12] According to research by Women's Aid, one in four women experience domestic violence in their lifetime. For women with a disability, this figure more than doubles.[13] As with non-disabled women, 'domestic abuse' is defined as being abuse at the hands of a current intimate partner or an ex-partner, but for disabled women this expands to include people in other trusted positions: family members, personal care assistants and health-care professionals.

Refuge, which runs forty-two refuges across twenty-three local authorities nationwide, tell me that a third of the women they assisted long-term in 2017–18 had one or more disability.[14] 'The disabled women we support report physical, sexual, coercive, psychological and economic abuse. We see many cases where the perpetrator is also the carer,' a senior manager explains. 'Exploiting their disability, perpetrators have opportunities to maintain greater control over their victims, keeping them isolated, stopping them working, denying or misusing medication, or preventing them from attending medical appointments. They also use their disability to humiliate them, threaten to have them sectioned or their children taken away.'

Go through the data and at every turn, disabled women are at greater risk of abuse and its consequences. Public Health England in 2015 found that disabled women, as well as being more likely to be abused, experience domestic abuse for longer periods of time, and more severe and frequent abuse than those without disabilities.[15] (Disabled men are also more likely to be victims than their non-disabled male counterparts but the role of gender means that it's still women with disabilities who are more affected. Disabled men experience a similar rate of domestic abuse as non-disabled women.[16]) Research by SafeLives found that disabled women are twice as likely to have attempted suicide following abuse (22 per cent) than non-disabled women, while studies also show that disabled women are twice as likely to suffer assault and rape.[17]

And yet there is little mainstream attention given to this crisis. I have never heard a politician discuss the needs of disabled women when talking about domestic violence, while there are few disability-specific refuges available despite disabled women being significantly more at risk than others. Beverley Lewis House in London, for example, is the only specialist refuge for women with a learning disability in the country. It's hard not to think that cultural attitudes towards disabled women have a hand in this. There's still a deeply embedded reluctance by society to acknowledge disabled people's sexual relationships; the asexualization ascribed to disabled women means that some don't associate us with being at risk of domestic violence, and if they do, the men with us can be perceived as – far from abusers – saints for 'putting up' with a disabled girlfriend. Such misconceptions around disabled women's lives can go to the heart of services meant to protect them; a two-year research project by the University of Kent's Tizard Centre in 2015 found that less than half of police officers in England, Wales and Scotland felt that women with learning disabilities were more at risk of domestic abuse.[18]

Moreover, it is not only that there is a lack of provision for disabled women, but also that there is limited awareness of what resources are out there. Talking to refuges and experts in the area of domestic violence or disability, I questioned them on the availability of support for disabled survivors. Each admitted they could not say how many refuges or services there were in the UK specifically designed for disabled women. 'Not enough,' as one put it.

Bethany first tried to leave her husband in 2008 once the children were older. But she found first-hand that being disabled made this even harder. 'I tried to find someone to help me,' she says. 'The council. Refuges. Nothing. It was all for hearing people.' Over the next eight years, Bethany made what turned out to be many thwarted escape attempts. At one point, she turned up at a refuge having left her husband only to be told they had no interpreters. Instead, she had to ask the staff for help by writing it down on bits of paper; summarizing her years of abuse in bullet points. The emotional toll alone meant it was hard enough to find the words but the language barrier made it impossible; like many Deaf people, BSL is Bethany's first language and she can't write well in English. 'I needed help but there was no one,' she says. In the end, she had to go back to her husband.

Research consistently shows that, as well as enduring higher rates of domestic abuse, disabled women experience more of these barriers to accessing support to escape, anything from the lack of a sign language translator for a Deaf survivor to a staircase as the only entrance for a wheelchair user.[19] Just one in ten domestic violence refuge spaces in the UK is accessible to people with physical disabilities, according to a BBC investigation in 2018.[20] Talk to those on the ground and inaccessibility is often cultural as much as practical; while many refuges stretch their limited resources to make adaptations to refuge accommodation and encourage outreach staff to consider disability, some staff often are not trained about the needs of survivors with disabilities. Effectively this means they are unable to support women when they need it most.

Marie tells me that, for example, the 'no-visitor' policy at refuges to protect residents can mean staff frequently do not let in interpreters, even if they have been paid for by a charity. Many refuges will not accept Deaf women at all, she says, citing concerns about 'health and safety', such as how someone might not hear a fire alarm or a doorbell. 'We loan equipment, like flashing doorbells, but some still say "no, we can't deal with that". And it puts Deaf women at risk.'

As local governments have seen their budgets squeezed,

provision for women escaping abuse has been another grim causality. Figures obtained under the Freedom of Information Act by the *Guardian* in 2018 found that refuges for women and children in England, Wales and Scotland had seen a funding cut of £6.8 million since 2010, amounting to an average cut for each refuge of £38,000.[21] The consequences are potentially deadly; a report by the Bureau of Investigative Journalism in 2017 found that more than 1,000 women and children have tried to leave their abusers only to be turned away from shelters in the last six months of the year,[22] with other studies finding that many refuges are turning away as much as 60 per cent of their referrals due to lack of space.[23] Specialist services are often the first to go, with some of the few facilities that existed for women with physical or learning disabilities closing their doors as austerity measures came in. In 2017, Women's Aid said almost a fifth of specialist refuges have now closed since the coalition first gained power.[24]

The cost-cutting has in many ways been defined by a push for councils to commission cheaper generic one-size-fits-all bed spaces for domestic abuse survivors in place of the security and expertise that come with refuge places. It's dangerous and short-sighted – only giving abuse survivors a roof over their heads rather than the psychological and practical support they need to rebuild their lives – but particularly so for those with additional needs, such as disabilities or language barriers. In 2016, Bethany was finally able to leave her husband – this time going to stay with her now-grown-up son and then her daughter. But when she asked her local council for help being rehoused in London, Bethany was told she was not a priority on the long social housing waiting list on the grounds she had technically chosen to leave her husband and home. Instead, she was given one option: a hostel. That would mean a Deaf abuse survivor being forced to sleep in a room next to men she had never met and whom she could not hear or communicate with. 'I couldn't explain it [to the council] because no one could understand,' she says.

Changes to the benefit system in recent years have made this harder still. As large-scale cuts to the 'welfare' bill kicked in after 2010, Kafkaesque bureaucracy and heavy restrictions have increasingly defined access to benefits. Universal Credit (UC) – the IT-based all-in-one system intended to replace the old benefit system by 2023 – is a key part of this, with both disabled people and domestic abuse victims two groups particularly affected (unlike the outgoing system, UC is paid to the main breadwinner, meaning male abusers can withhold money from their victims). In 2018, an influential group of MPs, the Home Affairs Select Committee, warned that Universal Credit rules were 'making it harder' for victims of domestic violence to leave abusive relationships and avoid economic abuse and control. The scandal meant that in January 2019 the new welfare chief, Amber Rudd, announced a u-turn allowing women to receive universal credit payments if they are the household's main carer.[25]

Victoria Harrison Neves from Refuge tells me the service is concerned that changes to the benefit system generally are now making it more difficult for women to leave their abusers, or even stopping them entirely. 'In our experience, Universal Credit [for example] can . . . limit the ability of women to save up even very small amounts to escape abuse, like a taxi to a refuge or relative's house,' she says. Even if a victim does manage to leave, further social security problems mean women – many who 'flee with little more than the clothes on their back' – often have to wait lengthy periods for their benefits.

To help her gain financial independence after leaving her husband, Bethany was advised to apply for Universal Credit but the process was foreign to her: she'd never used a computer before but was expected to apply online, had to wade through complex paperwork despite BSL being her first language ('It was so wordy,' she says), and had to set up her own banking as her husband shared her bank account. Even reaching the helpline was blocked because of her disability. Bethany had to ask her son to keep phoning the DWP to get support but officials often refused to talk to him on his mum's behalf, even after he explained she was Deaf. In the end, her son passed the phone over and said, 'Use your voice so they can tell you're Deaf, mum.' It took the best part of a year and intervention from DeafHope support workers and her son, as well as a sicknote from her GP, for Bethany to get her benefits.

It meant that even when she gained a one-bed flat with the help of her children, Bethany had to borrow money from them in order to feed herself while she waited for her social security to come through. The flat was unfurnished and she had nothing to her name but a television and a bed. 'I had to save for a year to buy furniture. Little bits,' she says. I ask her what she did without chairs and a table. 'I'd just sit on the bed all the time.'

In the end, after two decades of abuse and with support from DeafHope, Bethany was able to rebuild her life. For seven weeks she attended workshops by the service – six to eight survivors with two interpreters – and wishes she were still attending them. Resources, though, are tight. DeafHope has recently lost its funding for the whole of Surrey, which means they can no longer support women in the area. They're still providing a service for London and the South East, but worry there's 'very little hope' for Deaf people experiencing abuse who live in the rest of the country. In a climate of ever-squeezed funding, Marie and her colleagues fear that provision for Deaf and disabled women is seen as a 'luxury.' 'When there's less to go around, a . . . marginalized, largely invisible population is naturally not top of the list.'

'It's a bit of a primal fear that your children will be taken and no matter how hard you fight, you can't get them back,' says Jemima, one of the staff at an advocacy and advice centre run by, and for, disabled people in south-west London. Jemima, who uses a pseudonym here to protect the identity of the women she helps, has seen this fear lived out a number of times in recent years and is at the forefront of what in many ways is the local effort to keep disabled mothers with their children.

Across the country, there's a growing pattern of children being removed by the state. The number of looked-after children in England in 2018 was the highest it has been since 1985.[26] One in five children under five are referred to childrens' services; adoptions are higher than in any other European country, and now stand at the highest level since data was first collected[27] (more than 90 per cent of which are done without the consent of the family, according to Legal Action for Women, a legal service and campaign group[28]).

There's a clear class bias to this. Research by Legal Action for Women in 2017 warned that low-income women are unjustly being separated from their children due to poverty.[29]

Charges of neglect are being used to 'punish' women for their 'unbearably low incomes.'[30] The Child Welfare Inequality project in 2017 found this class difference to be so severe that children living in the poorest neighbourhoods of the UK are almost ten times more likely to be taken into care or placed in a child protection plan than those from affluent areas.[31] This is not surprising: parenting is much harder if you don't have enough money to provide food, housing, heating and clothing.

The influx of deep cuts to services since 2010 has only exacerbated this trend, with the Association of Directors of Children's Services (ADCS) in 2017 stating that austerity policies were 'fuelling record numbers of children being taken into care'.[32] It pointed to 'welfare' cuts, reductions in family support services such as Sure Start, and rising poverty levels as contributing to 'families find[ing] themselves at the point of crisis with little or no early help available'.[33] This is compounded by the fact that poorer local authorities – facing greater overall demand for child protection services and proportionally larger funding cuts – are increasingly rationing expensive early intervention services that might have previously caught problems before they turned into a crisis. In 2018, the charity Action for Children found that council budgets for early help services designed to prevent families reaching crisis point have shrunk by £743 million in five years – amounting to a cut of more than a quarter.[34] The pressure to cut early intervention services is likely only to increase in the coming years; the Local Government Association estimates that children's services will face a £3.1 billion funding gap by 2025 just to maintain the current levels of threadbare service.[35]

However, the reality for disabled mothers and their children is rarely considered. There's a significant gap in data monitoring the risk of disabled women unjustly losing access to their children, but what we do know is deeply concerning. For example, parents with learning disabilities are fifty times more likely to have their children removed from them and taken into care than their non-disabled counterparts.[36] Similarly, there is a noticeable lack of research on the impact of cuts on disabled women's right to raise a family, despite disabled women anecdotally being particularly vulnerable to losing access to their children, especially if they are also from a BAME background and working class. After all, being a disabled mother means you are considerably more likely to be taking on caring responsibilities or coping without a wage, particularly if you're a single parent.

Research by the disabled feminist organization Sisters of Frida in 2017 showed that disabled single mothers are 50 per cent less likely to be employed than non-disabled single mothers.[37] This risk of poverty has only increased in recent years as disabled mothers have faced vast cuts to disability services and benefits; the UK Women's Budget Group calculate that disabled lone mothers stand to lose more than £7,000 per year by 2021[38] – that's over a quarter of their income – due to a decade of cuts. That figure rises to over £10,500 (32 per cent of their income) if they have a child with a disability too.[39] These are mothers who already have to navigate day-to-day life with poor health and unequal access to services, often while being perceived as inherently less capable simply by virtue of being disabled.

Historically, disabled people in Britain – and with it, disabled mothers – have been largely viewed as unfit to give birth or to raise children. The sort of stigma that often faces work-ing-class women – that they 'breed too much', leach off soci-ety and are ineffective parents – has long been levelled in a different way at disabled women, who are routinely seen as defective females, asexuals and unnatural mothers.

Throughout the early twentieth century, such long-stand-ing ableist attitudes combined with the rise of the eugenics movement across Europe and the United States to go as far as to attempt to prevent disabled people from procreating. In 1907, the Eugenics Education Society was founded in Britain to campaign for sterilization and marriage restric-tions for the 'weak' in a bid to prevent what they saw as the degeneration of Britain's population. It was an open attempt to wipe out future disabled people from the country, with supporters claiming disabilities such as dwarfism, deafness and even minor defects like a cleft palate could be perma-nently removed from the gene pool, and, moreover, that this would be entirely preferable.

This was not a fringe belief, but rather went to the heart of the British establishment. While giving evidence before the 1908 Royal Commission on the Care and Control of the Feeble-Minded, Sir James Crichton-Brown recommended the compulsory sterilization of people with learning disabili-ties and mental health problems – an act supported by Winston Churchill.[40] In 1931, Labour MP Archibald Church proposed a bill in Parliament for the compulsory sterilization of certain categories of 'mental patient'.[41] Such legislation never passed in Britain, but it is believed that many forced sterilizations were carried out on disabled people under various forms of coercion.

Almost ninety years later, there has clearly been

considerable progress, with British disabled women of my generation largely able to embark on motherhood if we choose. This is no small progress considering that developed nations such as Japan only recently ended their sterilization of some disabled women in the mid-1990s,[42] while Australia still continues the practice, which falls under the United Nations definition of torture.[43] However, while the extremism of eugenics is no longer present, British culture still holds deeply regressive attitudes around disabled people and sexuality and, in turn, disabled women's ability to have sexual relationships or raise children. It's not uncommon for visibly disabled mothers to be questioned in the street by complete strangers if they're out with their children, be it asking if their son or daughter is 'really' theirs or how she had them.

These attitudes can seem low-level prejudice, but it would be naïve to think they did not come with consequences – particularly in times of austerity. The assumption can exist, even among professional bodies, that mothers who have disabilities are inherently less equipped to raise children than non-disabled parents, while at the same time – in an era of vast cuts to social care, housing and benefit budgets – the disabled women who are in need of practical support to suitably care for their children are increasingly denied it.

Carla called social services herself because she worried she was a bad mother. The twenty-seven-year-old has autism and multiple mental health problems – borderline personality disorder, depression and anxiety – as well as scoliosis of the spine and an immune system disorder. Her six-year-old daughter, Harmony, is disabled too; she has ADHD, epilepsy and a learning disability that leaves her with the reading age of a toddler.

It's just her and Harmony at home: at first, a privately rented small attic flat in London. To get to it, the stairs were so steep that both Carla and her daughter repeatedly fell down them. It was so cramped there were no cupboards to keep their things. When Carla was in the middle of a mental health flare, the flat was the first place to show the signs of things going awry: clutter everywhere, toys on tables, and clothes piled in corners. Depression meant Carla had no energy to clear it up. 'I got to the point I was looking around the flat and thinking, "my mental health must be really bad",' she says. 'I felt like I was a really bad mother. I didn't want Harmony to have to live in this mess.'

On top of the housework, Carla was struggling with day-to-day tasks for Harmony: making phone calls, getting to appointments and taking her to school on time. Going to new places is impossible for her without support because of her mental health and autism, she explains. 'I just can't do it.'

In 2016, Carla contacted her local council to ask for support – a few hours' social care for cleaning, she hoped, or some help with Harmony's school appointments. She cried on the phone but was informed social care wasn't available to support her. 'It was, "no, we only help people who can't get out of bed or who have an IQ below 70,"' she says. Over the course of a year, she repeatedly rang both adult social services and child social services for help but was refused an assessment. 'I was at rock bottom. I was falling and falling but if they'd helped me earlier [it wouldn't have got that bad],' Carla says. 'I know there's cuts but . . . what if you can't stand up for yourself? What if they make you cry and you just don't go back?'

This is common; cash-strapped local authorities are often

failing to provide a social care assessment for disabled mothers even when need is obvious. Research funded by Disability Research on Independent Living and Learning (Drill) in 2018 painted a disturbing picture. It found that adult social services too often ignore the needs of disabled people who become parents, frequently prioritizing 'monitoring' over the sort of meaningful, practical support that might keep families together.[44] The research, by the Tilda Goldberg Centre for Social Work and Social Care at the University of Bedfordshire, found that children's social services too often see the parent's disability as a potential risk to their children.

In the end, the council finally sent Carla an assessment pack: a large pile of complex paperwork she didn't understand. 'I said to them, "I have a disability. I need help with these forms," but they wouldn't give me any.' It was only when she went to Jemima's support centre and they helped her with the application that she got some state support: a social worker for herself from adult services and a child social worker for Harmony.

It was help from them that meant Carla was moved onto band A on the social housing list and moved into a ground-floor housing association flat. 'That was a big help,' she says. But there was little support after that. She was promised respite care for Harmony two days a week and some short breaks in the holidays – just a breather for when Carla needs a rest – but that did not materialize. Carla applied for 'minimum hours' for cleaning support – two hours a week – for when her mental health was at its worst, but was refused, she says. The state of the house 'was one of their main concerns. But they wouldn't do anything to help.'

Carla has only seen her social worker once. In place of a social care package, the worker had been ringing round local charities to see if a voluntary support worker could help Carla get out of the house. 'It just never happened,' she says.

As cuts to social care, housing and disability benefits have kicked in, there are reports that more disabled women have had to fight authorities for custody of their children, particularly after they had repeatedly been turned down for support. It can be a case of 'disabled women are not supported with their needs and then blamed for not parenting "properly",' explains Jemima. 'There's a real fear that social services will take the children instead of helping.'

Ellen Clifford, a manager at Inclusion London, a disabled-people-led disability service, tells me this has been exacerbated by benefit cuts and a social care system that's 'being cut to the bone'. 'I've attended case conferences with disabled women who have serious physical and mental health impairments and due to the fact that her needs are not being met [by her local authority] her children are being put on the "at risk" register,' she says. 'Because [of severe cuts], disabled women won't get support to fulfil their roles as mothers and carry out the domestic and childcare tasks they need support to do.'

Jemima tells me of a young woman called Jessica (not her real name) who had two children and was living with her wider family. Jessica, who had memory problems and trouble retaining information, was sent to a parenting unit by social services and accused of neglect: from not brushing the children's hair to having the bathwater too hot. Jessica clearly might have benefited from support, including help with finding more suitable housing and a care plan, such as visual reminders to help her get in a routine with the children. But she was given nothing. 'Catch-22,' Jemima says. 'She was deemed incapable of parenting, but not "disabled enough" to have support.'

In the end, Jessica's children were forcibly adopted. Jemima's agency did all they could to support Jessica but she became severely depressed and struggled to understand court proceedings. No post-adoption support was provided by the state, Jemima says, including help to write the two annual letters Jessica was allowed to send her children. 'So she doesn't.'

'It] is a power imbalance. Really, once you've been told you're not fit to have them, and there is no way for you to prove the council wrong, the whole system is stacked against you,' she says. 'Even saying you want to keep your children can be used to prove you don't recognize what is "best for them".'

The memory of that case is traumatic, Jemima admits, but what disturbed her as much was the realization that the charity alone cannot stop it being repeated again and again. 'We watched it happen,' she says. 'It felt like it could happen to anyone.' Any one of us with a disability.

Sarah's daughter was seven when she began caring for her mother. Sarah was pregnant with her third child at the time and started to struggle to walk. Seven-year-old Georgia would sit with her mum to comfort her as she rested, something that increased as Sarah's health worsened. The doctors called it symphysis pubis dysfunction, but really it means pain: her pelvis is 'stretched', and by 2016 it had got so bad that she needed surgery to fuse her pelvis back together with metal forced through the bone.

An occupational therapist from the hospital visited the family in North Yorkshire before Sarah's operation and provided aids for the bungalow: a commode, a shower stool and a 'grabber' to help Sarah reach the cupboards from her wheelchair. That was the extent of the help from the state. There was no agency care worker offered by the council or even mention of a social care assessment.

Instead, it was Georgia who picked up the slack: bringing tablets to Sarah, preparing food, and then taking it to her mum in bed. Sarah, now thirty-six, developed repeated bone infections after the surgery, and just as Georgia started secondary school, her daughter's caring role only increased. 'It's generally from morning till bedtime,' Sarah says of the situation now.

Money problems have had a domino effect to increase Georgia's caring hours. Early on in her illness, Sarah had to give up a wage as a human resources worker. As debts started to mount, she and her husband, Mick, went to their local Citizens Advice to see what help they could apply for. They were told they were only eligible for one disability benefit, Personal Independence Payment – anything else, like tax credits, were cut off as Mick's earnings as a printer took them over the low-income threshold. Sarah did not even qualify for out-of-work sickness benefits, despite the fact she was too ill to work. Again, Mick was said to earn too much and her maternity pay also ruled her out. 'I was so cross. We thought, "People get ill all the time. What do you do?"' she says. 'They just leave you. The children don't even qualify for free school meals.'

To try and get by, Mick started to take on more hours. He already worked full-time but took on nights and weekends for the overtime. It means he often is not there to help Sarah with the kids in the morning, so if she is not well enough to drive, her own mum takes the three of them into school. Otherwise, Georgia takes on the brunt of it: waking her brothers for school and making everyone's breakfast. 'Sometimes my mum can't move to simply get up in the morning,' Georgia says. 'I quietly wake my brothers so she can stay in bed and can rest.'

Most days, Georgia spends two to three hours caring for her mum fitted around the school day. In the holidays, that goes up to four hours. Often, Sarah is too unwell to get round the kitchen so Georgia is the one who makes dinner for the family. Jacket potatoes. Noodles. She's big enough to use the grill for cheese on toast now, Sarah explains. 'Like playtime to her. "What shall we make for dinner today?" '

Sarah's health fluctuates, which means Georgia's caring responsibilities do too. Sarah often struggles to sleep – multiple cushions prop up her painful pelvis – and on the nights she can't, she needs Georgia more the next day. When Sarah is at her worst her daughter has to help her wash in the shower. 'She even empties my commode for me.'

The term for someone like Georgia is a 'child or young carer', but I would call it a political euphemism for the safety net gone wrong. The last census in 2011 found there were 178,000 young carers (five to seventeen years old) in England and Wales.[45] That's eight-year-olds stretching to reach the high supermarket shelves for the weekly shop and thirteen-year-olds learning to make beans on toast for tea. This number is largely agreed to be a significant underestimate, with charities consistently placing the figure at more like 700,000.[46]

Many families with a disabled parent don't want to be 'on the record' that their children are undertaking caring roles, in part because of the stigma. There is also a fear the authorities may perceive them as not coping, while some children find it difficult to ask for help because they themselves fear being taken into care. Research carried out by *BBC News* and University of Nottingham in 2018 was extrapolated across England to correspond to more than 800,000 secondary-school-age children carrying out some level of care.[47] This constitutes a hidden underage workforce doing the jobs many adults would find a struggle. Of those, the survey suggested that more than 250,000 young carers are carrying out a 'high level of care', with 73,000 taking on the highest amount of care.[48]

The phenomenon of children caring for their disabled parent isn't a new one but it has been rapidly increasing in recent years. This includes the very youngest infants; census data published in 2013 showed that the number of five- to seven-year-olds carrying out caring responsibilities in England had reached almost 10,000 – an increase of around 80 per cent over the preceding decade.[49] As austerity spread and the squeezed social care system underwent cuts of billions of pounds, the number of recognized young carers in the UK rose by more than a third between 2013 and 2017.[50] Analysis by the *Independent* shows an additional 10,000 children and young people qualified to receive the carer's allowance in that four-year period.[51] Again, this is likely to be only a small snapshot of what's happening behind closed doors as only people over the age of sixteen are eligible for Carer's Allowance. Georgia, for example, doesn't count.

Sarah noticed how Georgia naturally stepped in to help

her at home when she first fell ill, despite only being at primary school. 'She's older than her years,' Sarah says. Still, the emotional toll is tough and Georgia sometimes feels lonely, anxious and isolated because of her caring duties, especially during the long holidays. She often does not want to go out with her friends, as she gets nervous her mum might need her at home, Sarah explains. Georgia's teachers know about the situation at home and she has learnt to be organized to be top of the class. When we talk during the summer, she'd already completed her homework on the first weekend of the holiday. She knew she'd be busy caring for the next six weeks.

In some ways, Georgia is bucking the trend. Research by the Children's Society in 2013 into the long-term impact of caring on a child's life found that one in five miss school because of caring responsibilities, and many do poorly in exams as a result.[52] Meanwhile the charity Barnardo's says child carers are less likely to go into higher education because of their caring roles, and are thereafter less likely to be able to get a steady and secure job.[53] If that wasn't enough, they are also much more likely to have mental health issues.

Sarah and Georgia are very close. Georgia will come and sit on Sarah's bed and cuddle, even now she is a teenager. This is clearly a loving, close-knit family – 'I couldn't ask for better kids,' Sarah says – but it is hard not to think that they are being let down by the authorities. Children like Georgia are, to all intents and purposes, being forced to pick up the caring roles the state has abandoned, and yet rather than outrage, this situation is greeted with a combination of resignation and applause.

Watch an annual *Children in Need* special or listen to most politicians and there is a concerted effort to promote the normalization of child carers – the social acceptance of a state of affairs that relies on a ten-year-old to make their sick mum's tea. As adult social care minister Caroline Dinenage put it in 2018, 'Young carers are this country's unsung heroes, tirelessly providing support for the people they love.'[54]

It is emblematic of the ease with which support for disabled people has been removed that we are even willing to use their children to plug the gap. The Care Act 2014, pegged as a major legal reform, in theory finally placed a duty on local authorities to consider the needs of children and young people living in households where there's an adult who has a disability or impairment. Young carers have a right to a 'needs assessment', which is supposed to determine whether the care they provide impacts on their health, well-being or education. But such warm words mean little when uttered at the same time as local councils are starved of the funds needed to implement them.

In reality, many young carers are not known to the authorities, or are left to carry on with their caring duties as they wait indefinitely even for an assessment. Research by the children's commissioner for England in 2016 found four out of five young carers who look after sick, disabled or addicted family members receive no support from local authorities.[55] The commissioner's survey of English local authorities found there were 160 carers aged under five, some of whom had been formally assessed and supported as carers.[56] This means that councils are fully aware that children as young as infants in reception class are acting as 'carers' in substitution for their parents' care assistants, but not necessarily that they are offering support. As one cash-squeezed council told the commissioner, 'We are essentially carrying out assessments as a tick-box exercise.'[57]

The danger is that, as cuts to services deepen in the coming years, the care burden shifted onto children is only going to further increase, while the normalization of it will mean it trundles on with little pressure for change. Local authority leaders warned the children's commissioner survey in 2016 that cuts to council funding meant resources were increasingly focused on children at risk of neglect or abuse – effectively meaning that support for other children, including young carers, would be severely limited.[58] Two years later, when a near bankrupt Somerset County Council launched proposals to try and stay afloat, it announced a £240,000 cut in help for young carers. It was only after local outrage that officials said the move would be 'deferred and reviewed'.[59]

Like many child carers, as things stand, it's a charity rather than the state that gives Georgia a break. Action for Children organizes days out for Georgia and her fellow young carers – theatre, trampolining and adventure play – as well as coming into her school for one-on-one counselling. It's a chance for her to have a confidential 'moan about me', Sarah smiles. The only problem is, she says, there are too many children who need help. 'There's so many [other child carers at the school], sometimes Georgia doesn't get to see the counsellor.'

CHAPTER 6

Children

Two years after David Cameron brought in the first wave of cuts, the *Daily Mirror* ran a front page featuring a picture of a child weeping from hunger to illustrate its story on food banks in Britain.[1] It quickly gained attention, becoming one of the most infamous media stories of the austerity age. This was partly down to controversy (it turned out it was in fact a picture of a child taken in San Francisco in 2009)[2] but also to how it unflinchingly depicted the harm that austerity policies were causing. Cuts that had previously widely been dressed up as cold economic prudence or a fair way of treating costly benefit scroungers were now human suffering brought to the breakfast table.

To put it another way, even the large swathes of the public who were content to support, say, benefit sanctions for the so-called feckless unemployed would likely pause at harming a child. In a climate that increasingly ranked our fellow citizens as undeserving, children were the definition of innocents – the last group in society many of us would choose to see go hungry. Sick and disabled children, by extension, in theory should garner this impulse even more. A society that professed to, at a minimum, always protect 'the most vulnerable' would surely not pull back support for disabled infants.

In fact, between 2012 and 2017 Britain's child safety net was repeatedly cut, from freezing child benefit to introducing the 'two-child-limit' child tax credits. To get a picture of how much progress this rolled back, the Resolution Foundation think tank calculates that by April 2019, for a second child, the benefit freeze introduced by George Osborne meant child benefit was worth less than when it was first fully introduced in 1979.[3]

Worse still, it was children with disabilities and chronic and life-limiting illnesses who took the brunt of such cuts, from the transition to Universal Credit to the loss of council tax allowance targeting parents of disabled children. The roll-out of Universal Credit alone will see a £175 million cut to child disability payments, with thousands of families with disabled children set to lose £1,750 a year under the new system.[4] The reality of such measures is ministers taking income from families who were already some of the poorest in the country. Any parent knows how expensive it is to have a child but this rockets if they have a disability. It is calculated to cost £215,553 to raise a disabled child to adulthood – 43 per cent more than for families with non-disabled children.[5] Parents are forced to find money for everything from wheelchairs to hoists, while often balancing their caring responsibilities around reduced hours (and pay) at work. A third of disabled children in 2018 subsequently live below the breadline – that's 400,000 kids – according to the Joseph Rowntree Foundation.[6]

Look behind the statistics and these are disabled children whose families are often barely able to afford food. Research by the charity Contact in 2018 into the costs of childhood disability found that 80 per cent of families had 'gone without' in the previous year.[7] This included children wearing scruffy clothes because their parents cannot replace them or missing out on hospital appointments because they could not afford the transport to get there. A quarter had skipped meals. A fifth had gone without heating. Four in ten had even gone without birthday or Christmas presents.[8]

Rather than social security being the safety net to catch them, the austerity age saw the so-called bloated 'welfare' bill begin to actively push these families further into hardship. Over a third of parents with disabled children surveyed by Contact in 2018 said that changes to benefits in the past two years had left their family worse off, with the large majority saying this was damaging their mental health and personal relationships. 'Benefits should be there to help people, not make us feel like scroungers and thieves. We are missing quality time with our terminally ill child all because of money,' said one parent. 'I am extremely worried about how me and my children will survive in this current environment. I feel that we have been sacrificed and scapegoated to pay for the financial crash,' said another. 'There is no one to fight on our behalf. The future is hopeless.'[9]

It's not hard to understand this fear. By 2021, the Equality and Human Rights Commission estimate an extra 1.5 million children will have been pushed into poverty as a consequence of the government's austerity programme, with disabled children among the worst-affected.[10] While the wealthy and healthy are largely cushioned, low-income families coping with disability are lined up for the biggest hit: households that include a disabled child are set to lose an average of £3,300 a year by 2021 once tax and benefit changes have been cumulated.[11]

Go to your local town centre and austerity is made visible. In the years after the recession, the exodus of the high street was a familiar sight; hollowed-out retail premises left vacant or replaced with pound shops and charity stores. A mile down from my house still sits a large pub last occupied almost a decade ago; windows boarded up and the golden title above its entrance now missing alternate letters. But if you want to really understand how austerity has gutted our communities look no further than the pulverization of services for children and young people.

Think of public spaces used by anyone from toddlers to teenagers and, odds are, it's been decimated by cuts. Hundreds of playgrounds have closed across England in recent years;[12] as an alternative, some councils have begun to issue a charge to play.[13] Youth centres across the country are disappearing as local authorities move to shred youth budgets by as much as 90 per cent.[14] A minimum of a thousand children's Sure Start centres – the cornerstone of the past Labour governments' social mobility drives – have closed their doors.[15] Swathes of libraries have followed suit – staffed by volunteers the odd day a week or morphed into centralized 'hubs' miles from neighbourhoods. Even parks – their budgets falling on average by 40 per cent since 2010[16] – are increasingly shut off from families as cash-strapped councils pull back maintenance or are forced to sell off green spaces entirely.

Few kids, though, have been hit harder than those with disabilities. While the number of disabled children in the country is increasing – standing at 33 per cent more than a decade ago[147] – fewer than ever receive support from the state. Research by the Disabled Children's Partnership, a coalition of sixty charities and organizations, in 2018 found a £1.5 billion funding gap for services needed by disabled children, resulting in tens of thousands missing out on help that might enable them to 'eat, talk, leave the house, have fun and attend school'.[18] Only a few months later, more than 120 national organizations, including children's charities, disability groups and teaching unions, joined forces to warn the government that services for children and young people were 'at breaking point', including healthcare, social services and education for disabled children.[19]

As if it was not enough that disabled kids were seeing their benefits shrink, deep cuts to local authorities were removing anything from health provision and social care to respite centres.

Satnam has put on two stone from stress since her daughter, Gurpreet, had her respite removed. Fifteen-year-old Gurpreet has a rare chromosome disorder resulting in learning and multiple physical disabilities: among them, five different heart conditions, chronic renal failure, double incontinence, partial blindness and hearing loss. She's been a patient at Great Ormond Street Hospital since she was born and has had seventeen surgeries over her young life, from open-heart surgery to spinal fusion. 'With all this going on, Gurpreet is the happiest, cheekiest girl you could meet,' Satnam, forty, says from her small town in Hertfordshire.

Satnam's husband was recently jailed for abusing her and it is just her at home to care for Gurpreet and her two other young children. It is a 24/7 job: feeding her daughter through a tube, changing her, giving her medications. On top of it all, the house is not accessible for Gurpreet's wheelchair so the living room acts as her makeshift bedroom: a special orthopaedic bed, surrounded by syringes, special feed bottles and changing equipment.

For fourteen years, the local respite centre, Nascot Lawn, has been, in Satnam's words, 'quite simply my family's lifeline'. Somewhere reliable with medical supervision that meant Satnam could take a break while knowing her daughter was happy and safe. While childcare and nurseries can be impossible for a child with disabilities, respite centres – filled with trained staff and a host of medical equipment – are often the only place a parent like Satnam can rely on. Every month, Gurpreet had four overnight stays at Nascot; a chance for Satnam to take her other two children to the seaside, to attend Gurdwara prayers to give her 'strength', or, as she puts it, 'to recharge and feel fresh and able to carry on caring'. A couple of months before I first speak to Satnam, Gurpreet has had complex surgery on both her feet – leaving her in double plaster from her toes to her knees that's only just come off. The time in the respite centre was Satnam's only break. 'I feel like for a few hours a weight is off my shoulders. I'm not constantly thinking ahead, feeds, bath, medicines,' she says. 'It kept me sane.'

But in the summer of 2017, the local clinical commissioning group told Satnam and the other parents that because of budget cuts they had to pull Nascot Lawn's annual £600,000 funding. Soon enough, Gurpreet's respite was cut down to only two nights across four months. In July 2018, it was stopped entirely.

For Satnam, the end of respite care 'felt like a dream I had woken up from'. It immediately impacted every aspect of her and her family's life. 'Having no proper scheduled, reliable, competent respite is like being on a merry-go-round continuously without stopping,' she says. Her parents do their best to help but both are in their late sixties and she is now constantly tired and emotionally strained. 'It really feels like my daily routines are never-ending. I can't plan anything. Caring non-stop is taking every ounce of strength I have.'

The centre's closure means Satnam has lost not only her only break but also the safety net for emergencies. When Satnam needed urgent surgery in 2015, it was Nascot Lawn that made it possible; they took Gurpreet in for four nights and then extra weekends to allow her mum to recover. 'Nascot was my back-up always,' Satnam tells me. 'Now we have nothing.'

What has happened to Gurpreet in Hertfordshire is being echoed across the country, with parents fighting local respite closures from Birmingham to Winchester. Since 2011–12, more than half of local authorities have cut spending on respite services for families with disabled children.[20] Take inflation into account and that shoots up to 75% of councils cutting their short-break provision in real terms.[21] A report by Contact in 2018 warned of the 'devastating impact of inadequate health and social care services' on families, calculating that a quarter of parents of disabled children provide 100 hours of care a week to plug the gap – equivalent to three full-time jobs.[22] In the coming years, the consequences could be devastating: the Disabled

Children's Partnership warned in 2018 that such severe lack of overall funding risks 'a tsunami of admissions' of disabled children having to go into residential care as unsupported parents cease to cope.[23]

It has resulted in a nationwide struggle between disabled children and the state that is meant to protect them. Families at their wits' end fighting for vital support from a system being starved of resources by central government. What's more, the fight to keep local respite centres open has happened at the same time as other services for disabled children, like school transport, are also being pulled. The law states that a child with a disability that prevents them walking to their nearest suitable school should get free transport help regardless of distance (non-disabled children must live more than three miles from their school to be eligible). But as cuts deepen, charities report that families whose child is clearly eligible for school transport are being refused help by their councils, while other local authorities are assigning unsuitable and unsafe transport to disabled children.

I spoke to a mother with a young son with physical and learning disabilities who lost his place on the school minibus with special seats, harnesses and trained guides. Instead, the council offered him a free bus pass by councils; that's a four-year-old wheelchair user who is non-verbal, incontinent, struggles to control his body and cannot understand instructions told to use a standard bus alongside commuters and students. The council only reinstated his specialist travel after an official appeal. Another told me of her young child being forced to take an almost three-hour round journey to school after specialist transport had been cut and parents were left in 'chaos'. The child arrived home distressed and sitting in soiled clothes.

This is the sort of inhumane and short-sighted cost-cutting that's come to characterize so many of the reductions to disability support. With safe transport, disabled kids can get an education while their parents can go to work and pay tax. Take the transport away, research by Contact in 2017 found, and almost half of parents, mostly mums, have had to reduce their working hours or not work at all simply because of school travel arrangements for their disabled child.[24]

Parents at Nascot Lawn opposed the closure of the respite centre for over a year; sleep-deprived mums and dads lobbying local officials, protesting outside council buildings, and even launching two successful judicial reviews. Still, the funding could not be saved and, after thirty years of serving the community, the centre shut its doors in November 2018. Without Nascot Lawn, Satnam has been offered alternative arrangements at another centre across the county. But it takes Gurpreet seventy-five minutes to get there on the school bus and the support hours work out considerably fewer than what Nascot provided. Worse still, staff there are not trained to provide even basic medical procedures, such as replacing the 'button' of the tube Gurpreet needs for food and liquids when it pops out. Instead, whenever this happens, the new centre will have to take her to the nearest hospital.

'Gurpreet has spent so much of her life in hospital that she becomes extremely worried, anxious and physically tries to gag when she goes to hospital,' Satnam explains. 'Because of her learning disability, it's very difficult to explain to her what is going to happen. If they took her to hospital, she would never want to go back to respite again.' Still, Satnam accepted the offer of a place at the new respite centre. She is terrified that if she turned down this option, she'd be left without any respite at all and would not be able to cope. When we next talk, Gurpreet has just had her first night at the new centre. 'She cried and kept asking for me,' Satnam says.

This is respite care in name only; rather than being able to have a breather, every time Gurpreet goes in for respite, her mum is effectively 'on call' in case she needs help. Gurpreet is due more surgery in a month – this time, a complex dental procedure – and despite her relentless efforts, the stress of it all on Satnam is clear.

Families like Satnam's often show a superhuman sort of strength but it's not hard to see that if the state cuts the support they rely on, they can become deeply vulnerable. Carers UK research in 2015 found that almost eight in ten family carers have anxiety and over half say they have depression as a result of their caring responsibilities.[25] In the years after austerity deepened, it was not unusual for me to hear from desperate carers; many of them losing access to local services or benefits and struggling to stay afloat. The suicide of thirty-three-year-old mother Jane Kavanagh reported in the *Daily Mirror* in October 2018 was one case that gained much attention on social media at the time. Jane was sole carer to her fifteen-year-old daughter, who needed 24/7 care due to a severe degenerative condition, but had no respite breaks, no social care, not even adaptations to her inaccessible house for her daughter's wheelchair.[26] In April 2018, she dropped off her daughter and other child at her parents'. A few hours later, her neighbours found Jane's body. As Satnam puts it to me: 'Austerity is punishing the wrong end of society. The fall-out from breaking us will be felt in the longer term.'

As recently as sixty years ago, educating disabled children in mainstream schools in Britain was still almost unheard of. Shipped off to so-called 'special schools', instead of being nurtured, their treatment was often abusive. In *Pride against Prejudice*, author Jenny Morris recounts the story of one disabled woman who spent her childhood living in various institutions in England in the 1940s and 1950s.[27] In one place, disabled children had to go outdoors at 6 a.m. every morning and weren't allowed to put bedclothes over themselves at night. For half the day they were not permitted to speak. When they were sick, they were expected to eat their own vomit. If staff took a dislike to a child they would hold her under the water in a bath until she started to go blue, while a group of children would be assembled to watch what was happening. On one occasion, the woman recounts, a staff member held a child under the water for so long that the child drowned.

Several decades on, disabled children in Britain were in many ways experiencing not only a safer society but also one that – on the face of it, at least – offers us a real education and the life chances that come with it. As a disabled child in the 1990s, I was able to flourish in education. A support worker, ramps, and lifts provided by my local authority in Lincolnshire enabled me to go to both a mainstream primary and secondary school and, along with my non-disabled sister, go on to be the first generation in my family to get a degree at university. Perhaps it's because of this very progress for people like me that it feels particularly painful to see the current state of our education system for disabled children.

Go to your local comprehensive in recent years and austerity is evident: teachers fundraising for paper and stationery, non-specialist teachers filling in to teach A level maths, school buildings leaking and crumbling around them,[28] or even closing their doors on a Friday afternoon because they can't afford to run a full school week.

But in the face of crippling budget pressures, it's special-needs support for disabled children that is particularly under threat. Against a backdrop of austerity and large cuts in government funding of local authorities, head teachers and charities warned in 2018 that 'children with the highest levels of need are paying the biggest price for the government's real terms cuts to education.'[29]

Take specialist support for Deaf children. Teachers of the Deaf are in many ways the difference between a Deaf child being locked out of school or blossoming – be it through helping children's communication skills, training other teachers, or even providing advice on hearing aids. Between 2014 and 2018, one in ten of these specialist teachers were cut, according to figures from the National Deaf Children's Society (NDCS), with local councils set to collectively cut support for Deaf children alone by a further £4 million by 2019.[30]

This is replicated across the board. While the number of disabled pupils has gone up, parents and teachers face a funding climate so squeezed that in 2018 the National Association of Head Teachers (NAHT) warned of 'a national crisis' affecting thousands of children with disabilities across the country, with the Local Government Association estimating a £1.6 billion funding shortfall for SEND pupils by 2020–21.[31] You only have to look at the rise in parents forced to challenge cuts to their child's support to get a picture of the scale of this; a *Guardian* investigation in 2018 found that the number of appeals heard by the special educational needs and disability tribunal nearly doubled between 2016 and 2018, with councils embarking on such unjustifiable cuts to support that families were successful in nine out of ten tribunal hearings.[32] Children who were not even born at the time of the financial crash were suddenly finding themselves told to take the burden, losing anything from their transport to get to school, to speech and language therapy, to teaching assistants who provide one-to-one support.

Such severe cuts to specialist provision are resulting in a large increase in the number of disabled pupils in specialist schools after these children are left without the practical support that can help keep them in mainstream schools; the number of pupils with special educational needs attending maintained special schools increased from 38.2 per cent in 2010 to 44.2 per cent in 2018, with a further increase in the number attending independent special schools.[33] This situation is so critical that, in 2017, the United Nations criticized the rising numbers of disabled children educated in segregated 'special schools' in the UK.[34] Sixty years on from the apparent phasing out of segregated education for disabled people in Britain, parents were now facing a choice between placing their child in a segregated school or a local, mainstream school that's too starved of funding to be able to adequately teach disabled pupils. For some disabled children, it means not going to school at all.

Nine-year-old Louis is taught in his front room. His disabilities are complex: among them autism, sensory processing disorder and dyspraxia. 'His brain doesn't get the information at the right time,' his mum, Joanna, explains from their home in Surrey. Louis wears ear defenders as his sensory processing disorder means he's acutely sensitive to sound – even the noise of a pen dragging on paper can hurt him – and he often spins to help his inner ear balance and to 'focus his brain'. When Louis became of school age, he was enrolled at a mainstream primary school in the borough but there was no specialist support in place for his disabilities. To school staff members not trained to help special-needs pupils, it seemed like Louis was just a naughty child acting out. 'They kept saying it was just bad parenting,' Joanna, forty-two, tells me. 'At one point the head teacher even said to me, "you've got to just train him, like a dog".'

For over a year, Joanna struggled to get the school to recognize Louis's disability and went as far as to bring in a child social worker to get a formal diagnosis. But it did no good. Just two weeks before his diagnoses appointment in 2015, Louis was excluded from the school at six years old – making him the youngest child in the borough to have been expelled.

It should come as little surprise that those vulnerable kids who are not given adequate health or academic support are often kicked out of school. Disabled children like Louis have long been victim of exclusions – pupils with special educational needs and disabilities (SEND) are up to six times more likely to be excluded from school and account for almost half of all permanent exclusions.[35] Class and race mean this burden is spread even more unevenly. In England, a black Caribbean boy on free school meals with SEND is 168 times more likely to be permanently excluded than a white British girl without SEND.[36] All too predictably, austerity has only exacerbated this situation. The National

Education Union (NEU) in 2018 warned that disabled children were increasingly at risk of being excluded from school simply because budget cuts meant they were not getting the help they needed. Their survey of 900 staff working in schools in England found that half of respondents' schools had cut support for special educational needs and disabilities this year, and nearly a third had cut SEND posts.[37]

As demand for specialist support soars and cash-strapped councils threaten bankruptcy, this is likely to only increase in the coming years. Across the country, many local authorities are taking a variety of desperate methods to survive the crisis, from overspending and plunging deeper into the red, to even robbing other educational budgets – such as early years' funding – to plug the special needs gap.[38] Louis's own home county of Surrey is on the precipice of deep cuts to support for disabled pupils, with the county council proposing to reduce its special-educational-needs budget by £20 million from 2018 to 2019.[39]

Schools are meant to receive additional funding to meet the needs of children with disabilities, but an NAHT survey in 2018 found that only 2 per cent of respondents reported that the top-up funding they were now receiving was enough to meet disabled children's needs.[40] There are around 1.2 million children recognized as having special educational needs, but the NAHT says that as many as a million of them appeared to have received no additional funding at all through their schools in 2018.[41] Joanna feels that Louis's school wanted him 'out' before he was officially diagnosed so that he did not 'eat into their funding'. 'If they had the funding for teaching assistants in mainstream schools, [children] wouldn't be excluded,' she says.

When funding is slashed, it sends a message about what disabled kids are worth. On top of exclusions, parents and campaigners tell me that some families with disabled children are now being discouraged from even applying to schools in the first place because head teachers know they will not be fully reimbursed for the cost, despite this being legally required. Others are being 'encouraged' to be home-schooled. The number of children with special needs being home-schooled in England, Wales and Northern Ireland jumped by 57 per cent between 2012 and 2017.[42] Meanwhile, government figures show that more than 4,000 SEND children were without a school place in 2017 – more than double the number of the year before. Campaigners say the real figure is far higher as official data doesn't include the many SEND pupils who don't have either a special needs statement or an education health and care plan (legally binding documents guaranteeing their rights to additional support). As it is, just 253,000 of the country's 1.2 million SEND pupils have care plans or special educational needs statements.[43] According to the regulator, Ofsted, two thousand children with the greatest needs who do have care plans were still awaiting provision in 2018 – three times more than in 2010.[44]

It's disabled kids who are being deprived of an education, but really this climate means we all lose something bigger. Attend a diverse school alongside disabled classmates and non-disabled children are more likely to grow up understanding disability and accepting difference. Siphon disabled children off to segregated schools or shut them away to be taught at home and it isn't unusual for non-disabled children to never come across a disabled person.

As things stand, some disabled children are disappearing from the school system altogether. A scathing report by Ofsted, in 2018, into the education of children with special educational needs and disabilities, found almost 5,800 pupils with SEND left their school between years 10 and 11; some of them will have been removed from the school roll illegally, because they were perceived as a 'risk to the league tables' by potentially bringing down the school's GCSE results. It amounts to erasing imperfect children, in which a target-driven culture mixed with cost cutting means special-needs pupils are either subtly discouraged to apply to a school or accepted only to be then excluded on tenuous grounds. Half of the 19,000 GCSE-aged pupils that dropped off school rolls between 2016 and 2017 never reappeared on another state-funded school roll.[45] The result is thousands of disabled children in limbo, cut out of the education system entirely.

Louis is one of them. At the point he was excluded, he was too young to go to another suitable school in the borough. It meant that he was at home for a year without a school place. Instead, a tutor popped in for brief lessons – at first 'just for play work', and after Joanna intervened some English and maths lessons. Joanna herself worked at a special-needs school but without a school place for Louis she had to quit her job to care for him at home. The knock-on effect has been to push the family into money problems. 'Things are hard financially,' she says. 'We just about get by but have no money spare. We live day to day,' she says. This is far from uncommon: a survey of parents and carers by the charity Ambitious about Autism in 2018 found that 30 per cent had been forced to give up their job as a result of school exclusions, with a further fifth having to go part-time.[46] This matters, not least because a low income is already inexorably linked with a family like Louis'. Being a special needs kid is both a cause and effect of poverty: research by the Joseph Rowntree Foundation (JRF) in 2016 shows pupils with a disability are more likely to experience poverty than others and are also less likely to leave school with outcomes that reduce the chances of living in poverty as adults.[47]

Louis was eventually offered a school place: an independent school for children with emotional and behavioural problems. It was wildly unsuitable – Louis has disabilities, not behavioural problems – and it cost the local authority over £70,000 a year, Joanna says. 'I think they [the council] put him in there because it was the only school that would take him.' If parents refuse a placement, it's not unheard of for them to be forced through the courts to enrol their child in residential boarding homes – 'Parents live in fear [of that]', Joanna says – and she reluctantly accepted the offer out of anxiety that Louis would be schooled away from home otherwise.

In fact, Joanna says, 'there were problems from day one.' Because it was a school for 'troubled' children with emotional problems, not disabilities, Joanna says staff weren't qualified to teach disabled pupils and had no understanding of Louis's diagnoses. Louis is high-functioning autistic – 'He's smarter than me,' Joanna says – but the school gave him remedial lessons. 'Like one plus one equals two.' Each afternoon, staff took the class out for an activity, like a ball pit. 'Even though I explained to them it would be sensory overload for him [and] he'll get distressed,' Joanna says.

In the classroom, Louis had no consistency – his class went through seven teachers in the space of a year – and he was regularly punished for struggling to cope with his surroundings. The punishment consisted of being locked up in seclusion rooms for up to three hours – 'It was a padded cell, basically,' Joanna says – and Louis was restrained if he struggled. 'Problem is, when you put a [disabled] child into that environment, they're going to have a meltdown,' Joanna explains. 'And the minute you put your hands on a child with autism, they think they're being attacked.' A seven-year-old held down by five adults is not a fair fight and Louis was left with bruising over his body.

Louis's mental health subsequently went downhill to the point where he told his mum he wanted to die and was regularly self-harming: hitting his head repeatedly and scratching his skin. Scared, Joanna went to her GP and was referred to Child and Adolescent Mental Health Services (CAMHS) but was told therapy was not available. Theresa May identified mental health provision as one of her 'burning injustices' that she pledged to tackle upon gaining power, but the service has seen deep cuts in recent years, none more so than for children.[48] Research by the Association of Child Psychotherapists and other professional bodies in 2017 found that a third of NHS children's mental health services 'face cuts or closure'.[49]

Meanwhile the NHS watchdog reported that children with mental health problems were waiting up to eighteen months to be treated.[50] An investigation by the Education Policy Institute (EPI) in 2018 found that referrals to children's mental health services in England had increased by 26 per cent over the last five years, but nearly one in four of those were rejected. This meant that at least 55,000 children were not accepted for treatment in 2017–18 alone, including young people who had experienced abuse or, like Louis, showed evidence of self-harm.[51] This is the inevitable result of more cuts: between 2010 and 2016, more than a fifth of local authorities had either frozen or reduced their CAMHS budgets every year; that's £85 million gone in six years.[52]

Without the safety net of NHS mental health services, Joanna put her energies towards getting Louis out of a school where he did not feel safe. By March 2018, Joanna had successfully challenged the local authority to terminate Louis's independent school placement. As a last resort, she requested a personal budget that allowed her to implement a home-schooling package. She was refused. Instead, Louis was just given another home tutor. He's now back to two hours a day of lessons at home. It is an education in the smallest sense. Louis loves science but he only gets funding for maths and English lessons.

Even now, at nine years old, his treatment at the behavioural school means that Louis has to sleep in Joanna's bed. He's scared of being alone. It feels, she says, like the council 'wrote him off at six'. It looks like Louis will be taught at home for the near future and Joanna doesn't even know if he'll get a secondary school placement. It means potentially years of not only Louis going without a proper education but also of the family going without a decent income now Joanna cannot get out to work. 'We look at the positives like we have food and a roof over our heads,' she says. '[We're] luckier than some as my mother helps us out financially for birthdays and Christmas.'

Listening to Joanna, it is hard not to think that there will be some sort of school revolt – where parents see their children shunned and ignored and say enough is enough. In fact, that is just what has happened. Parents in Surrey have started a legal challenge over the county council's planned cuts to the special-needs budget. The week we spoke, Joanna had hoped to go down to the court herself to show her support but ended up at the dentist when Louis needed a tooth out.

This sort of battle – busy parents taking on cash-strapped councils – is being replicated up and down the country, with parents anywhere from Bristol or North Yorkshire to the London borough of Hackney initiating legal action against multimillion-pound cuts to special-needs funding. It is a David-and-Goliath fight on paper – many of the parents are having to crowdfund online to even afford the legal fees – but it's providing a shot of hope. In 2018, Bristol city council was forced to cancel planned cuts of £5 million to its SEND budget after a court ruled the council had acted illegally,[53] while Hackney backed down on plans to change funding arrangements.[54]

In Surrey, Joanna is struggling to even get Louis an updated needs assessment; now nine, he hasn't had one since he was six. A new report is vital if he has any hope of being given a mainstream school place 'but that costs money too so they won't do it.' Joanna knows the cuts mean there are many parents in the borough whose children aren't in the educational system – as she puts it, 'You fight for the diagnosis thinking that will be it, that you'll get support. You then find out there are no services' – and is currently organizing a meeting at the nearby rugby club where parents can lobby the local MP.

What really frightens her, she says, is that Louis and other disabled children like him are going to be 'these kids that's left and left and left'. 'I've seen it too many times at work,' she says. 'Sixteen and no qualifications. No apprenticeship because no one will take him because of his exclusion. Then into society with no services.' Louis wants to be a doctor, she says. 'He doesn't stand a chance.' Currently, after all, he doesn't even have science lessons.

Louis's generation of disabled children are in many ways experiencing the sharpest end of what I would call the equality myth. In some ways, they are at a significant advantage compared with previous generations: where it was once culturally expected – and entirely legal – to segregate or exclude disabled people from education, jobs or transport, a disabled child growing up today does so in a Britain that largely tells them they will be treated equally. But this increasingly feels like a cruel false promise, one that on paper dangles unprecedented opportunity and independence for the next generation of disabled people, but in reality oversees polices that are regressively pulling back their rights and life chances. Unflinching, Joanna sums it up: 'They're forgotten children. That's what they are.'

Conclusion

British compassion for those who are suffering has been replaced by a punitive, mean-spirited, and often callous approach.

United Nations rapporteur Philip Alston,
November 2018

The active, deliberate and persistent maltreatment of Britain's disabled people has gone beyond critical levels. Over the course of a decade, people with disabilities, chronic illness and mental health problems have been routinely driven into destitution, pushed from the workplace and stripped of the right to live in their own homes. The gains that generations of disabled campaigners fought for have been rapidly rolled back, and the promise that the Great British welfare state would always protect disabled people shown to be little more than a fantasy.

Societies generally accept that we have a collective duty to provide a safety net for citizens in times of ill health or disability – that's why we have the NHS, disability benefits and equality laws. As this book has shown, it is not simply that Britain is now shirking those responsibilities. It is that we have reached a point where we are practically relishing it, in which a cocktail of austerity and long-standing prejudice towards disabled people is leading to the sort of large-scale negligence that at its extremes is tantamount to abuse. The British state has to all intents and purposes turned on the very people who are most in need of its help.

The increase in disability hate crime in recent years – from which even disabled children have not been exempt – shows, at its most extreme, the toxic attitudes bolstering such unprecedented cuts. The people on the very bottom rung of society have been shrewdly dehumanized by those at the top. Smearing disabled people as idle, fakers and abnormal makes it more and more difficult to empathize with them. The stories of the disabled people this book has told show at first hand the consequences: how the rationale that people affected by disability and poverty are 'not quite like other human beings' has come to excuse and normalize any number of nightmarish results that, even a few years ago, would likely have been unthinkable.

As ministers prepare to further demolish the safety net relied on by millions of disabled and working-class families, all at a time of the colossal change of Brexit, the time has rarely been more ripe for a new kind of solidarity politics – one that recognizes the humanity and contribution of disabled people, and rebuilds the public's trust in a flourishing welfare state.

After all, some of the biggest issues facing domestic politics in the upcoming years will uniquely impact disabled people, while reverberating across society as a whole. Near-bankrupt local councils are ceasing to meet even their legal duties, with the social care system for disabled and older people on its knees. Affordable-housing shortages, mixed with haemorrhaging living standards, have created a modern epidemic of homelessness and insecurity, in which disabled renters are at the sharpest end. The multi-billion-pound mass roll-out of Universal Credit is set to bring with it widespread destitution and even added risk of suicide,[1] as continual cuts to social security and an increasingly hostile climate abandon the sick and disabled.

What is both bleak and a source of hope is that it is entirely within Britain's power to fix this. Far from being inevitable, inequality for disabled people is avoidable. The transformation in disability rights over the latter half of the twentieth century came about as a result of concerted efforts to improve the lives of disabled citizens. On the other side of the coin, the increase in hardship for disabled people over the past decade is a direct result of political choices. Britain can stop disabled people going hungry, if we have the will.

This will is building. While immediately after the global crash the narrative that austerity in Britain is both necessary and – even – morally right was widely accepted (a narrative the Labour Party crucially failed to challenge), recent years have seen this dogma start to lose its clout. Theresa May's declaration at the 2018 Conservative Party conference that 'austerity is over' was widely meaningless – as this book has shown, more deep cuts are due in the coming years – but the fact that she felt the need to say it was not. Opinion polls consistently show the public to be weary of austerity. The British social attitudes survey in 2017, for example, showed that public tolerance of government cuts is collapsing, with 48 per cent of people surveyed supporting higher tax and more spending, up from 32 per cent at the start of austerity in 2010.[2] Notably, there was a surge in support for spending on disabled people, with 67 per cent supporting funding for disability benefits, compared with 53 per cent in 2010. There was also a significant softening in attitudes to benefit recipients, with the proportion of people believing that claimants were 'fiddling' the system dropping between 2015 and 2017 from 35 per cent to 22 per cent – its lowest level in thirty years.

It is time to seize on this shift to make the case for a rejuvenated twenty-first-century social safety net, and, with it, strengthened disability rights. The most effective way to tackle inequality of disabled people is to think about it in the round, looking at issues of housing, employment, social security and social care, and offering a coordinated strategy that not only is right morally but also speaks to everyday common sense. The left is often criticized for supposedly outlandish spending pledges, while conservatives position themselves as arbiters of prudent economics. This myth has rarely been peddled more effectively than through the austerity era, when the vast removal of state support was sold to the public as some sort of shrewd financial management. In fact, while arguing there was 'no money' to meet disabled people's needs, successive Conservative chancellors found cash for tax cuts for corporations and the rich: while austerity policies since 2010 will have cut social security benefits by £35 billion a year by the early 2020s, tax cuts will cost the Treasury £47 billion per year by 2021–2.[3]

What's more, policies which pull support from disabled people have both a terrible human and literal cost. Take away the social care assistant who helps a wheelchair user get dressed, and that person can no longer work and pay tax. Cut the housing benefit that helps a mum with MS and her kids stay in their accessible home, and the council has to pick up the temporary-accommodation bill. The left should never sideline the human consequences of austerity – indeed, creating a compassionate climate where such suffering matters is crucial – but our argument can only be strengthened by beating Conservatives on their own terms. Far from deep cuts to disabled people's support being economically prudent, it is actually costing us more to plaster over errors than to invest in long-term solutions.

To that end, we need to tackle how the social safety net is seen. Austerity has demolished not only funding for the welfare state but also the principles behind it. Too often, it is now viewed as a draining cost to keep down rather than a world-class strategy to provide security in our times of need. Across the board, the benefit system is in chaos, with disabled people forced through a system defined by hostility and humiliation. The 'tick-box' testing by multi-billion-pound private companies rolled out by the coalition government has been uniformly proven to be grossly negligent (as of 2018, as many as 70 per cent of appealed benefit rejections were overturned), while causing widespread poverty and mental health crisis. Social security assessments for disabled people must be taken out of profit-driven hands and brought back 'in-house', with decisions based on evidence provided by the disabled person's own doctors. It gives an insight into how hysterical the mistrust of 'faking' disabled people has become that the state trusting their medical notes could be seen as radical.

Next, we must get to grips with disability and work. Attempts to reduce the disability employment gap have made snail's-pace progress in decades, with recent ministers using the zealous rhetoric of getting people 'off the sick' while doing little to address the actual barriers that keep disabled people out of work and cut off from the security of a regular wage. Indeed, through cuts to schemes like Access to Work, they have made it actually harder. The arguments used by right-wing politicians to push people off benefits are in some ways correct: people are (largely) financially better off in work, while there can be consider-able psychological benefits to a fulfilling job. But they completely neglect the relevant questions. Where are all these jobs that are suitable for disabled or chronically ill people? Who are the bosses willing to hire a worker whose heavy fatigue, say, means they can only work half-days or who needs to repeatedly take time off for medical appoint-ments? Similarly, such critics often ignore the fact that, for disabled workers, taking an unsuitable job can be consider-ably worse for their health than no job at all. This is even more the case in a labour market that is increasingly char-acterized by insecure, low-paid and unrelenting casualized work. The push for a four-day week by some unions and campaigners in recent years gives hope that narratives around working conditions are becoming more mainstream – a shift that would benefit non-disabled and disabled colleagues alike. In the meantime, normalizing flexitime, job sharing and remote working would be a positive step. Overall, governments need a strategy that understands how to assist disabled people who can take a job with the right support, while accepting – and providing a dignified safety net for – disabled people whose health means they will never be able to do paid work.

This sort of nuance is more often than not missing from the conversations around disability. The easiest thing in the world for those in power is to simply blame the individual – for their poverty, their unemployment, even their own illness. The left has not done a good enough job in recent years of communicating the structural causes behind disabled people's struggles. Moreover, no one has done a good enough job of addressing the structural causes behind non-disabled people's struggles. To put it another way: it is no real surprise at a time of squeezed wages, unaffordable homes, diminishing life chances and growing uncertainty that the average voter has had little desire to think of their disabled neighbour. Or, worse, that they are ripe for duplicitous voices to tell them that the cause of their woes is not, say, insecure jobs or a lack of social housing but the costly 'welfare' bill. It is difficult to focus your energy on what is happening in a care home to a disabled stranger when you're struggling to pay the bills, or your children can't find afford-able housing. The challenge in the coming years is to bridge this gap, to show not only that disabled people are not an economic threat, but also that the struggles facing each of us are not so different after all.

A favoured idiom of some disability campaigners is describing non-disabled people as 'the not yet disabled' – essentially skewering the very human but false belief that ill health will only ever hit *other* people, and instead establish-ing that it could befall any of us at any time. The rationale is logical: if the public understood that, for example, bad luck means that they too could become too disabled to work, they may be more likely to care when out-of-work sickness benefits are cut. But in some ways, this argument surely gives up the ground we're trying to win. Public backing for a well-funded safety net won't be secured when non-disabled people care about disability benefits because they may one day need it themselves, but when they care because someone else needs it now. Besides, the cuts that early on were pitched as solely a concern for disabled people have in time come to the doors of the rest of the public. From unprecedented local council cuts, to Universal Credit's mass roll-out, to the effects of Brexit, in the coming years austerity's reach is only going to spread. To turn George Osborne's infamous phrase around: increasingly, we really are all in this together.

One of the greatest challenges in any of this is how disabled people are perceived. Long-standing cultural prejudice around disability, teamed with the demonizing rhetoric of austerity, has exacerbated a sense of difference in British society: an othering that suggests that disabled people aren't quite normal, or want a life – family, home or education – like everyone else. These attitudes do not exist harmlessly in a vacuum but are directly related to how willing non-disabled people are to see state programmes for disabled people destroyed. Why improve the lives of people who don't want a family or home like anyone else? What's the point in funding social care if disabled people don't go to the pub with friends or need to get to the office like 'normal' people?

Part of this surely comes down to representation, in culture as well as politics. Put it this way: a non-disabled person is much more likely to empathize with a disabled person who's had their social security cut if they've grown up surrounded by positive, everyday versions of disability – be it on-screen, in the media or at school or the office. Similarly, disabled people's needs are significantly more likely to be addressed if we are in positions of power ourselves, from more disabled MPs in the House of Commons to disabled people being at the forefront of disability charities and think tanks. As it stands, only a handful of MPs are disabled, for example – meaning disabled people are effectively excluded from the decision-making bodies that so often determine our fates.

The kind of history that seems to dominate our culture is too often centred on the concept of a benevolent ruling class bestowing rights upon marginalized groups. This has been particularly prevalent when it comes to disabled people – a group who have long been viewed as passive, weak, as infants in need of 'looking after'. But as this book has shown, disabled people are the ones who know their own lives, and it is their voices that should be amplified in a society that so often tries to speak for us. Disabled people, like the working class, have organised throughout the decades to gain our rights and – as these rights are threatened afresh – it is disabled people who are front and centre of the fight back.

Progress is not a straight line. It ebbs and flows; it flourishes and strains. Despite decades of progress, the intricate threads that make up disabled people's safety net are always vulnerable to those in power who wish to cut them away. As successive generations, it is up to each of us to remake the case for state support for disabled people as a fundamental right. It is not hyperbole to say that the stakes have rarely been higher than now.

Britain feels increasingly like it is at a tipping point, a precipice of national character in which we decide what sort of society we want to be. Brexit, for its part, threatens to push us not only from precious resources but also from the energy and focus to address the pressing issues of the day. The risk of carrying on as we are is clear – creeping poverty, the hollowing out of public services, and a growing gulf between the ultra-rich and the disabled and poor. This book has disability at its heart, but it has always been about something more. After all, a society that is content to see wheelchair users queuing at food banks has not only lost its way in how it treats disabled people, but also abandoned its basic humanity. As the welfare state teeters on the edge of collapse, there has never been a more crucial moment to find our compassion and social solidarity – to strengthen the social safety net, demand more from our leaders than austerity, and reject policies led by callousness and fear. The rallying cry for our times is clear: how things are is not how they need to be. Disabled people's lives depend on it.

AFTERWORD

A Fairer Society in the
Age of Coronavirus

There is a joke among those who make a living writing about politics that, in these times of 24/7 news, you could spend years on a book only for events to change within weeks of publication, quickly making the text irrelevant. When I wrote *Crippled*, my worry was quite different – that it wouldn't become irrelevant. In late 2018, I concluded that we were in many ways at a crossroads in British society: we could stay as we were and continue on the path of inequality and individualism or we could take a leap for real change, in which a society of equality and solidarity could see more disabled people have the opportunity to lead full and dignified lives.

Within six months of publication, British politics found itself faced with that stark choice. A winter general election, pushed through by a Brexit logjam, saw two very different pitches put to the electorate. On the one hand, the Labour Party offered a radical programme of universal services, from blanket social care for the over sixty-fives (with an eye to extending it to younger disabled people) to free university tuition. On the other, the Conservatives drilled home a 'Get Brexit Done' message and words of support to the NHS.

When Boris Johnson was caught by a journalist burying photographic evidence of a sick child in his pocket in the final days of the campaign, there could hardly have been a clearer symbol of what this particular prime minister really thought of public services. The reality that this book outlined – a crumbling NHS, vilified social security system, squeezed wages, and growing homelessness – suddenly did not so much seem a story of the present or even the past, but a glaring warning for the future.

In the end, a general election that was ultimately defined by Brexit but also plagued by anti-Semitism, muddled communication, and a polarizing leadership saw Labour crash to its worst defeat since the 1920s and Johnson's Conservative Party returned with a landslide majority; in turn, the UK finally left the European Union. The increase in donations made to food banks and emergency housing in the immediate days after the election result gave a hint at the trepidation some of the public felt.[1] Far from a wave of hope for disabled people, the years ahead were suddenly signalling a further attack on the welfare state and, with it, continued poverty and isolation, all on top of the uncertainty surrounding the fallout from Brexit.

We need only look at the events of the following months

to see where such a choice has taken us. Life expectancy stalled for the first time in more than 100 years and even reversed for the most deprived women in society, largely thanks to austerity measures.[2] Meanwhile people in poorer areas have more of their lives blighted by ill health than their wealthier counterparts.[3] Universal Credit threatened to push people with mental health problems into destitution, as an appeal court ruled the government's benefit cuts were discriminating against disabled people.[4]

Post-Brexit immigration rules were introduced with plans to ban low-paid migrant workers – a move that unions warned would 'spell absolute disaster' for the social care sector.[5] Boris Johnson's adviser was forced to quit over his support for eugenics, as the so-called culture war engulfed people with learning disabilities.[6] Elsewhere, the Department for Work and Pensions (DWP) was caught 'pressuring' vulnerable and disabled people to accept 'deals', paying thousands of pounds less in benefits than they could be legally entitled to.[7]

Barely a month after the Tories were re-elected, the death of Errol Graham, who starved to death after having his disability benefits stopped, dominated the headlines. The fifty-seven-year-old had severe social anxiety and struggled to leave the house but nonetheless had his social security removed when he missed his fit-for-work assessment. The story encapsulated not only the human cost of the broken benefits system that *Crippled* warned of but the casual cruelty that is caused when the social safety net so many rely on goes wrong. Bailiffs only discovered Graham's emaciated body when they knocked down his door to evict him. When he was found, his Nottingham flat had no gas or electricity. The only food in the kitchen was two tins of fish, four years out of date.[8] He weighed four and a half stone.

Meanwhile, the emergence of the coronavirus pandemic further jolted political life as we knew it. The whole of society was impacted by the spread of the virus and efforts to stay safe, from the retail sector to the self-employed, in an unprecedented lockdown of social activity. But this hit few harder than people with underlying health conditions. After all, public health emergencies are not equal opportunity events: the poorest, most marginalized and disabled are generally worst affected, while the wealthy, connected and healthy are better able to cushion themselves.

Disabled people simultaneously found themselves at greater risk of coronavirus while least likely to be able to access food and medicine as many were forced to shield at home for months. At the same time, the impact of emergency coronavirus legislation sparked concern among many disability organizations for what the years ahead would look like. The bill most notably temporarily removed the legal duty on councils to provide social care to all who are eligible, as well as making it easier to section people into mental health facilities, and to keep them detained there for longer periods.[9]

Disabled people who were already enduring a stripped-down care service after years of cuts now faced a further loss of rights. At the same time, emergency measures to shield citizens from the economic fallout of the pandemic by bolstering the social security system noticeably missed out many disabled people; charities warned that hundreds of thousands of disabled and chronically ill people subsequently faced being pushed into poverty as the coronavirus raged.[10]

It would be easy to feel defeated at this point. Indeed, it is not only understandable to feel overwhelmed in such times – it is entirely human. But if I could be presumptive enough to offer a lesson from the writing of *Crippled*, it would be this. Illness is scary. Poverty is arduous. Uncertainty worries us all. It is wrong – and ultimately unhelpful – to sanitize this, to put a false gloss on it, to pretend everything is okay. The very least people who are suffering deserve is to have their suffering known, not least because it is the only way those in power will ever be forced into doing something to address it.

And yet there is always hope. There is hope in the temporary nature of things; a political landslide will be overturned in due time. There is hope in organization; in the union that raises a cleaners' wages or the welfare team who wins a cancer patient's benefits back. There is hope in solidarity; that we are not alone, even when it feels like it.

In the spring of 2020, as the UK's coronavirus lockdown began, 500,000 volunteers signed up to the NHS to give their time to those in need. It was an army of helpers, doing everything from driving people to hospital appointments to dropping off food parcels to the isolated. This was on top of informal, local mutual aid groups that sprung up all over the nation in a bid to reach people with a disability, as well as the elderly, who were forced to self-isolate to protect themselves from the virus.[11] This volunteerism in many ways reflected a trend that has come to define so much of the austerity era, where food banks and community groups have been left to patch up the holes left by a shrinking government.

Yet what was fascinating about the response to the coronavirus was how mutual aid was accompanied by something else: the growth of the state. Established truths were suddenly turned on their head. With businesses forced to close, billions of pounds of loans were offered to bosses while employees who couldn't get to work were granted 80 per cent of their wages. Private landlords were banned from evicting tenants during the crisis, while local authorities in England started housing all rough sleepers – as if it had been possible all along. Middle-class professionals suddenly found themselves reliant on the social security system as nearly a million people applied for universal credit after being made jobless from the lockdown.[12]

A global pandemic had forced Britain's small state Conservative party to opt for mass intervention. The sort of large-scale investment formerly dismissed as a 'magic money tree' or dangerously 'Marxist' was now common-sense pragmatism. The deep cuts to public services and squeezes on wages were, it seemed, a political choice after all.

It was not only our relationship with institutions that changed during the coronavirus crisis but how we viewed the people in them. Low-waged supermarket workers and care staff previously dismissed as unskilled and unimportant were suddenly the heroes of the hour, while ministers who had formerly starved hospitals of funds found themselves clapping NHS staff along with a grateful nation.

For all the lab work and vaccine hunts, it is ultimately society itself that pandemics put under the microscope.

Where does power sit? What is the role of the state? When the crunch comes, are we protected? The coronavirus, for its part, laid bare the frailty of Britain's social contract after a decade of cuts – public services that had been starved of funding, millions of people in insecure and low-paid work, and a social security system unfit for purpose. In turn, it shone a light on some long-ignored truths: universal health-care is a non-negotiable good; workers dismissed as unskilled are actually the ones who keep us alive; public services are precious resources to be invested in for hard times; each of our lives is more dependent on others than we may think.

Perhaps few areas showed this more than the welfare state. If *Crippled* outlined what can happen when the safety net is devalued and shredded, the coronavirus pandemic was an unforgiving reminder of why it need be valued and protected. The pandemic fallout quickly exposed the myths at the heart of government cuts in recent years: that the welfare state is not actually a drain or a burden but a precious form of collective insurance against life's challenges, be it ill health, disability, or unemployment. As the writer Peter C. Baker put it on life after coronavirus, 'Disasters and emergencies do not just throw light on the world as it is. They also rip open the fabric of normality. Through the hole that opens up, we glimpse possibilities of other worlds.'[13]

We have already seen such glimpses. They are there in the public's newfound respect for the lowest paid who have fed and nursed them through a pandemic. It is there in a right wing government forced to invest in public services, provide income for the sick and unemployed, and house the home-less. It is there in the general population beginning to view social security as something no longer just for 'other people'. Or to put it another way: it is there not in the crisis, but in how we choose to rebuild after it.

The task for the Left going forward is to ensure the transformative actions we have witnessed are not temporary, but a turning point that long outlives the immediate crisis. The drastic measures governments have taken in recent months, not only in Britain but around the world, are evidence of just how much the state can accomplish – that there is really no limit to the changes that can be made, or the interventions that can be waged, if there is sufficient public demand for it. To return to a key sentiment of this book: where we are is surely not the best we can do.

The coming years will undeniably present great challenges to Britain as we are set to fight on three fronts. Brexit remains a great uncertainty squarely focused on the marginalized as any economic impact will inevitably hit the poorest. The coronavirus likely risks creating a recession of its own, all while the nation's infrastructure from libraries to social care must recover from a decade of austerity. This is on top of the juggernauts of the climate crisis and rampant economic inequality that our global neighbours face with us.

And yet out of the ashes can rise more than a flicker of light. Improved sick leave. Higher wages for care workers. Greater empathy for the disabled and ill. A culture of collectivism based on our interdependence. Strengthened and newly respected social security. The possibilities for progress are in many ways endless, only limited by the scale of our own vision. Those of us with egalitarian ideals in Britain are now tasked with some of the greatest challenges we could imagine, but with each challenge comes a chance for change.

The dark era in which we find ourselves does not mean only that a vision of hope and ambition is still possible for the left – it is more important than ever. We can achieve it, together.

Nottingham, May 2020

Notes

Introduction

1 Patrick Butler, 'UN inquiry considers alleged UK disability rights violations', *Guardian*, theguardian.com, 20 October 2015.

2 Jason Beattie, 'United Nations says treatment of disabled people in the UK is a "human catastrophe"', *Daily Mirror*, mirror.co.uk, 31 August 2017.

3 Patrick Butler, 'UN panel criticises UK failure to uphold disabled people's rights', *Guardian*, theguardian.com, 31 August 2017.

4 *BBC News*, 'PM David Cameron: London Paralympics will inspire', bbc.com, 29 August 2012.

5 George Osborne, 'George Osborne's speech to the Conservative conference: Full text', *New Statesman*, newstatesman.com, 8 October 2012.

6 Simon Duffy, 'A fair society? How the cuts target disabled people', the Centre for Welfare Reform, centreforwelfarereform.org, January 2013.

7 *Full Fact*, 'The Sun's benefit fraud figures need context and clarification', fullfact.org, 1 March 2012.

8 Martyn Brown, 'Iain Duncan Smith: "We'll root out the benefits cheats who pretend to be ill for money"', *Daily Express*, express.co.uk, 30 December 2014.

9 Robert Booth, 'One in five Britons with disabilities have their rights violated, UN told' *Guardian*, theguardian.com, 7 October 2018.

10 Dan Bloom 'Tory welfare cuts have hammered the disabled declares Britain's human rights watchdog', *Daily Mirror*, mirror.co.uk, 25 October 2018.

11 BBC News, 'Theresa May: People need to know austerity is over', bbc.co.uk, 3 October 2018.

1 Poverty

1 Joseph Rowntree Foundation, JRF analysis for Frances Ryan, 2018.

2 Ibid.

3 Equality and Human Rights Commission (EHRC), 'Being disabled in Britain: a journey less equal', socialmetricscommission.org.uk, 2017.

4 Scope press release, 'Sky-high energy costs leave disabled people out in the cold', 2017.

5 EHRC, 'Being disabled in Britain: a journey less equal'.

6 The Social Metrics Commission, 'A new measure of poverty', lif.blob.core.windows.net, September 2018.

7 Helen Barnard et al., 'UK Poverty 2017', Joseph Rowntree Foundation, jrf.org.uk, 4 December 2017.

8 Ibid.

9 The Living Wage Foundation, 'The calculation', livingwage.org.uk, 2018.

10 Jon Stone, 'The DWP is cutting a disability benefit that already leaves a third of recipients struggling to afford food', *Independent*, independent.co.uk, 8 December 2015.

11 The New Policy Institute (NPI), 'Disability and poverty', npi.org.uk, 11 August 2016.

12 Ibid.

13 Heriot-Watt University for the Joseph Rowntree Foundation, 'Destitution in the UK', jrf.org.uk, June 2018.

14 Ibid.

15 Patrick Butler, 'Destitution is back: And we can't just ignore it', *Guardian*, theguardian.com, 3 July 2016.

16 Ibid.

17 Patrick Butler, Matthew Taylor and James Ball, 'Welfare cuts will cost disabled people £28bn over five years', *Guardian*, theguardian.com, 27 March 2013.

18 Patrick Butler, 'Welfare spending for UK's poorest shrinks by £37bn', *Guardian*, theguardian.com, 23 September 2018.

19 Claudia Wood, 'The government has a duty to assess the impact of its benefit cuts', *Guardian*, theguardian.com, 27 March 2013.

20 Scope and Demos, 'The hardest hit of the hardest hit', scope.org.uk, 26 March 2013.

21 Channel 4 News Online, 'Disabled people "hit by multiple benefit cuts"', channel4.com, 27 March 2013.

22 Simon Duffy, 'A fair society? How the cuts target disabled people', the Centre for Welfare Reform, centreforwelfarereform.org, January 2013.

23 Andrew Hood, Agnes Norris Keiller and Tom Waters, 'Significant cuts to two parts of the benefit system to be phased in from next week', Institute for Fiscal Studies, ifs.org.uk, 30 March 2017.

24 BBC News, 'Universal Credit: Charities' disability benefits warning', bbc. co.uk, 17 October 2012.

25 Equality and Human Rights Commission, 'The cumulative impact of tax and welfare reforms', equalityhumanrights.com, 14 March 2018.

26 Robert Winnett, '500,000 to lose disability benefit', *Daily Telegraph*, telegraph.co.uk, 13 May 2012.

27 BBC News, 'Disability living allowance replaced by PIP scheme', bbc. co.uk, 8 April 2013.

28 BBC News, 'Disabled benefit delays "a fiasco", say MPs', bbc.co.uk, 20 June 2014.

29 Work and Pensions Select Committee, 'PIP, ESA trust deficit fails claimants and the public purse', parliament.uk, 14 February 2018.

30 May Bulman, 'Nearly half of disabled people reassessed under Government's new benefit system had financial support withdrawn or reduced', *Independent*, independent.co.uk, 14 December 2017.

31 Robert Winnett, '500,000 to lose disability benefit', *Daily Telegraph*, telegraph.co.uk, 13 May 2012.

32 Rowena Mason, 'Benefit reforms will end "something-for-nothing culture", says Duncan Smith', *Guardian*, theguardian.com, 1 October 2013.

33 Peter Walker, 'Benefit cuts are fuelling abuse of disabled people, say charities', *Guardian*, theguardian.com, 5 February 2012.

34 Simon Walters, 'I will go after the bogus disabled – some of them DO get better', *Mail on Sunday*, dailymail.co.uk, 30 March 2013.

35 Will Worley, 'Disability benefits should go to "really disabled people" not "anxiety sufferers", says Theresa May's adviser', *Independent*, independent. co.uk, 26 February 2017.

36 Scope, 'Extra costs: The financial penalty of disability', scope.org.uk, 20 February 2018.

37 Scope, 'Sky-high energy costs leave disabled people in the cold', scope.org. uk, 13 January 2017.

38 Money Advice Centre and CACI, 'One in six people in the UK burdened with financial difficulties', moneyadviceservice.org.uk, 19 September 2017.

39 Scope, 'Disabled people and financial well-being: Credit and debt', scope.org.uk, July 2013.

40 Ibid.

41 Scope, 'Financial crisis deepens for disabled people', scope.org.uk, 22 July 2013.

42 Citizens Advice, 'Doorway to debt', citizensadvice.org.uk, 19 March 2018.

43 Alex Campbell, 'Benefits changes: Warnings as crisis loans scrapped', BBC News, bbc.co.uk, 29 March 2013.

44 Ibid.

45 Patrick Butler, ' "Local welfare" schemes in England on brink of collapse, says report', *Guardian*, theguardian.com, 14 October 2018.

46 Ibid

47 Patrick Butler, 'Homeless? Here, have a tent . . .', *Guardian*, theguardian.com, 3 June 2013.

48 University of Oxford and the Trussell Trust, 'Financial insecurity, food insecurity, and disability', trusselltrust.org, June 2017.

49 Ibid.

2 *Work*

1 Frances Ryan, 'David Clapson's awful death was the result of grotesque government policies', *Guardian*, theguardian.com, 9 September 2014.

2 Ros Wynne Jones, 'Family of soldier David Clapson who died after benefit sanctions lodge formal demand for inquest', *Daily Mirror*, mirror.co.uk, 1 November 2016.

3 Claudia Tanner, 'Diabetic woman, 27, died after slipping into a coma when her benefits were stopped and she "couldn't afford to eat"', *i News*, inews.co.uk, 11 October 2018.

4 Sophie Borland, 'This bloke is on the sick! Angry GP cites Hawking to shame hordes of patients asking him to sign them off', *Daily Mail*, dailymail.co.uk, 2 August 2013.

5 Benefits and Work, 'Coalition wages war on disabled with 580% increase in ESA sanctions', benefitsandwork.co.uk, 13 August 2014.

6 Ben Baumberg Geiger and Demos, 'New research sets out how a better WCA is possible', demos.co.uk, 20 February 2018.

7 Dan Bloom, 'More than 5,000 sick and disabled benefit claimants have been sanctioned for 6 months', *Daily Mirror*, mirror.co.uk, 17 August 2017.

8 The University of York et al., 'WelCond project', york.ac.uk, 22 May 2018.

9 Ben Baumberg Geiger and Demos, 'New research sets out how a better WCA is possible', demos.co.uk, 20 February 2018.

10 Patrick Butler, 'Benefit sanctions: The 10 trivial breaches and administrative errors', *Guardian*, theguardian.com, 24 March 2015.

11 John Pring, 'DWP sanctions claimants "by any means necessary", MPs are told', *Disability News Service*, disabilitynewsservice.com, 17 May 2018.

12 *Liverpool Echo*, 'Esther McVey says benefit sanctions "teach" job seekers to take hunt for work seriously', liverpoolecho.co.uk, 20 November 2013.

13 Patrick Butler, 'Put universal credit on hold to protect disabled claimants, say MPs', *Guardian,* theguardian.com, 19 December 2018.

14 Dan Bloom, 'More than 5,000 sick and disabled benefit claimants have been sanctioned for 6 months', *Daily Mirror*, mirror.co.uk, 17 August 2017.

15 National Audit Office, 'Benefit sanctions', nao.org.uk, 30 November 2016.

16 Ben Baumberg Geiger, 'Benefit "myths"? The accuracy and inaccuracy of public beliefs about the benefits system', *Social Policy and Administration*, 17 September 2017.

17 Patrick Butler, 'Charities urge ministers to drop planned cuts to work support allowance', *Guardian*, theguardian.com, 27 October 2015.

18 Jay Watts, 'No wonder people on benefits live in fear. Supermarkets spy on them now', *Guardian*, theguardian.com, 31 May 2018.

19 Martyn Brown, 'Iain Duncan Smith aims fresh broadside at UK's sick and disabled', *Daily Express*, express.co.uk, 24 August 2015.

20 *Daily Express*, 'Crackdown on sick-note culture will help the UK', express. co.uk, 23 August 2015.

21 Jonathan Portes, 'Welfare savings and incapacity benefits', National Institute of Economic and Social Research, niesr.ac.uk, 16 April 2015.

22 The National Audit Office, 'Contracted-out health and disability assessments', nao.org.uk, 8 January 2016.

23 William McLennan, 'Man ruled "fit for work" dies from heart attack on way home from job centre', *Camden News Journal, camdennewjournal.com*, 20 January 2017.

24 Kevin Clark, 'Hartlepool man found dead on beach after sickness benefits stopped', *Hartlepool Mail*, hartlepoolmail.co.uk, 17 August 2017.

25 Stewart Carr, 'Disabled Luton woman "hounded" for benefits claims', *Luton Today*, lutontoday.co.uk, 18 May 2018.

26 B. Barr et al., ' "First, do no harm": Are disability assessments associated with adverse trends in mental health? A longitudinal ecological study', *Journal of Epidemiology and Community Health*, 2016, 70, 339–345.

27 Luke Traynor, 'Benefit cuts blind man committed suicide after Atos ruled him fit to work', *Daily Mirror*, mirror.co.uk, 28 December 2013.

28 Hannah Fearn, 'Government fitness for work test is making disabled people sicker, report claims', *Independent*, independent.co.uk, 3 March 2015.

29 Jonathan Portes, 'Welfare savings and incapacity benefits', National Institute of Economic and Social Research, niesr.ac.uk, 16 April 2015.

30 Oliver Wright, 'DWP fit-to-work assessments cost more money than they save, report reveals', *Independent*, independent.co.uk, 8 January 2016.

31 Press Association, 'Disabled benefit claimants to get extra £1.7bn after underpayments', theguardian.com, 17 October 2018.

32 National Audit Office, 'Investigation into errors in Employment and Support Allowance', nao.org.uk, 21 March 2018.

33 Nick Sommerlad, 'Disabled benefits blunder means 15,000 died before getting share of £970million' , *Daily Mirror,* mirror.co.uk, 19 December 2018.

34 EHRC, 'Being disabled in Britain: A journey less equal', equalityhuman-rights.com, 3 April 2017.

35 National Autistic Society, 'The autistic employment gap', autism.org.uk, 21 February 2017.

36 BBC News, 'Learning disability employment rate "unacceptable"', bbc.co.uk, 4 December 2015.

37 Sonali Shah and Mark Priestley, *Disability and Social Change*, Policy Press, 2011. p. 121.

38 Ibid.

39 Office of National Statistics, 'A08: Labour market status of disabled people', ons.gov.uk, 13 November 2018.

40 John Vale and Georgina Stubbs, 'Theresa May reveals plan to get one million more disabled people into work', *Independent*, independent.co.uk, 30 November 2017.

41 Victoria Wass and Melanie Jones, 'A tale of two commitments: Tracking progress on disability and employment', Cardiff Business School, disability-atwork.co.uk, 2017.

42 Scope, 'Disabled people shut out of job market due to workplace bias', scope.org.uk, 28 September 2017.

43 Leonard Cheshire, 'Seven out of ten disabled workers failed by employers' leonardchesire.org, 21 February 2019.

44 Randeep Ramesh, 'Only 3.5% of people referred to Work Programme find long-term jobs', *Guardian*, theguardian.com, 27 November 2012.

45 Employment Related Services Association, 'New report finds gap between government ambition and reality for supporting disabled jobseekers', ersa.org.uk, 24 October 2016.

46 Ibid.

47 Work and Pensions Select Committee, 'The future of the European Social Fund inquiry', parliament.uk, 4 April 2018.

48 Emma Munbodh, 'DWP to shut 68 Jobcentres across Britain with 750 jobs at risk – The full list of branches affected', *Daily Mirror*, mirror.co.uk, 7 July 2017.

49 Office for National Statistics, 'Internet users in the UK', ons.gov.uk, 19 May 2017.

50 Gov.uk, 'Strategy seeks one million more disabled people in work by 2027', gov.uk, 30 November 2017.

51 Scope, 'Disabled people fear losing their jobs and hide impairments to stay in work', scope.org.uk, 14 February 2017.

52 Scope, 'Data reveals government will fail on pledge to get one million more disabled people into work without rapid action', scope.org.uk, 1 September 2017.

53 Tarani Chandola and Nan Zhang, 'Re-employment, job quality, health and allostatic load biomarkers: Prospective evidence from the UK Household Longitudinal Study', *International Journal of Epidemiology*, 2018, 47(1), 47–57.

54 Papworth Trust, 'Facts and figures 2018: Disability in the U.K.', 2018.

55 S. Longhi, 'Research report 107: The disability pay gap', Equality and Human Rights Commission, equalityhumanrights.com, August 2017.

56 Ibid.

57 Nicholas Watt and Patrick Wintour, 'Welfare reform minister: Some disabled people "not worth" minimum wage', *Guardian*, theguardian.com, 15 October 2014.

58 Nicola Slawson, 'Philip Hammond causes storm with remarks about disabled workers', *Guardian*, theguardian.com, 7 December 2017.

59 John Pring, 'Labour MP told to quit influential post after "offensive" minimum wage call', *Disability News Service*, disabilitynewsservice.com, 21 September 2017.

60 Channel 4 News, 'Disabled people "should work for less", says MP', channel4.com, 17 June 2011.

61 John Pring, 'Duncan Smith refuses to apologize over 'exploitative' comments', *Disability News Service*, October 25 2018.

62 EHRC, 'Measuring and reporting on disability and ethnicity pay gaps', equalityhumanrights.com, 15 August 2017.

63 Papworth Trust, 'Facts and figures 2018: Disability in the United Kingdom', 2018.

64 EHRC, 'Being disabled in Britain: A journey less equal', equalityhumanrights.com, 3 April 2017.

65 Leonard Cheshire and ComRes, 'One in five employers say they would be less likely to employ a disabled person', leonardcheshire.org, 14 December 2017.

66 Papworth Trust, 'Facts and figures 2018: Disability in the U.K.', 2018.

67 BBC News, ' "Shocking" disability access to shops', bbc.co.uk, 6 December 2014.

68 Gwyn Topham, 'Bus services in "crisis" as councils cut funding, campaigners warn', *Guardian*, theguardian.com, 2 July 2018.

69 GMB, 'Thinking Differently at Work' neurodiversity campaign, gmb.org. uk, October 2018.

70 Scope, 'Disabled people fear losing their jobs and hide impairments to stay in work', scope.org.uk, 14 February 2017.

71 Public Interest Research Unit, 'New study finds workplace hell for disabled workers', dpac.uk.net, 30 April 2015.

72 Scope, 'Disabled people fear losing their jobs and hide impairments to stay in work', scope.org.uk, 14 February 2017.

73 Scope, 'Current attitudes towards disabled people', scope.org.uk, 1 May 2014.

74 *Guardian*, 'Editorial: The Guardian view on legal aid: Cuts have caused chaos and must be reversed', theguardian.com, 12 August 2018.

75 Frances Ryan, 'Disabled workers can't afford justice to deal with workplace harassment', *Guardian*, theguardian.com, 6 January 2016.

76 Ibid.

77 Owen Boycott, 'Legal aid cuts creating two-tier justice system, says Amnesty', *Guardian*, theguardian.com, 11 October 2016.

78 Anushka Asthana, 'Number of legal aid providers falls 20% in five years, figures show', *Guardian*, theguardian.com, 19 September 2017.

3 Independence

1 Heather Stewart and Denis Campbell, 'Theresa May pledges to seek long-term solution to social care squeeze', *Guardian*, theguardian.com, 14 December 2016.

2 John Pring, 'Government's social care plans side-line needs of working-age people' *Disability News Service*, disabilitynewsservice.com, 23 November 2017.

3 *Gov.uk*, 'Community care statistics: social services activity, England – 2015 to 2016 report', gov.uk, 5 October 2016.

4 Leonard Cheshire, 'The state of social care in Great Britain in 2016', leonardcheshire.org, 23 November 2016.

5 Scope, 'Disabled people's experiences of social care', scope.org.uk, no date 2015.

6 Patrick Butler, 'UN panel criticises UK failure to uphold disabled people's rights', *Guardian*, theguardian.com, 31 August 2017.

7 Care and Support Alliance, 'Disabled people left without the care they need, in breach of the law', careandsupportalliance.com, 24 October 2018.

8 Ibid.

9 Local Government Association, 'Councils take over 1,000 people to court for "social care debt"', local.gov.uk, 6 June 2018.

10 Ibid.

11 Local Government Association, 'LGA launches own green paper as adult social care reaches breaking point', local.gov.uk, 31 July 2018; Andy Bounds, 'Local councils to see central funding fall 77% by 2020', *Financial Times*, ft.com, 4 July 2017.

12 Southwark Carers, 'Meals on wheels under threat as more councils drop service due to cuts', southwarkcarers.org.uk, no date 2016.

13 Ibid.

14 Patrick Butler, 'New "big society" bid to boost charities' role in public services', *Guardian*, theguardian.com, 8 August 2018.

15 Ibid.

16 Steven Swinford, 'Women will have to give up work to look after parents unless EU care workers are given priority after Brexit', *Daily Telegraph*, telegraph.co.uk, 5 August 2018.

17 Patrick Butler, 'East Sussex council set to cut services to bare legal minimum', *Guardian*, theguardian.com, 3 August 2018.

18 Frances Ryan, 'We must help the disabled people facing imprisonment at home', *Guardian*, theguardian.com, 15 May 2014.

19 BBC News, 'Disabled people win living fund case against government', bbc.co.uk, 6 November 2013.

20 BBC News, 'Independent Living Fund closure ruled lawful', bbc.co.uk, 8 December 2014.

21 Inclusion London, 'One year on: Evaluating the impact of the closure of the Independent Living Fund', inclusionlondon.org.uk, 5 September 2016.

22 Jessica Elgot, 'Disability activists block House of Commons entrance in cuts protest', *Guardian*, theguardian.com, 19 July 2017.

23 Victoria Brignell, 'When the disabled were segregated', *New Statesman*, newstatesman.com, 15 December 2010.

24 Ibid.

25 BBC Lancashire, 'Forty years of Chronically Sick & Disabled Persons Act', bbc.co.uk, 21 May 2010.

26 In Control, 'Independent living survey 2016', in-control.org.uk, 21 November 2016.

27 Ibid.

28 May Bulman, 'NHS cost cutting leaving disabled people "interned" in care homes', *Independent*, independent.co.uk, 25 October 2017.

29 Ibid.

30 EHRC, 'NHS facing court action over unlawful policies', equalityhuman-rights.com, 19 March 2018.

31 MS Society, 'Younger people with MS stuck in care homes for older people', mssociety.org.uk, 14 November 2017.

32 May Bulman, ' "I've been wearing the same pyjamas all year": Plight of care home residents laid bare in damning report', *Independent*, independent. co.uk, 9 May 2018.

33 BBC News, 'Winterbourne View: Care workers jailed for abuse', bbc.co.uk, 26 October 2012.

34 May Bulman, 'Care home staff convicted after disabled residents were "kicked, punched and stripped naked" ', *Independent*, independent.co.uk, 8 June 2017.

35 UCL, 'Neglect common in English care homes', ucl.ac.uk, 21 March 2018.

36 Women's Budget Group, 'Investing 2% of GDP in care industries could create 1.5 million jobs', wbg.org.uk, 8 March 2016.

37 BBC News, 'National Audit Office asked to look into Motability', bbc. co.uk, 8 February 2018.

38 Nick Parker, 'Free BMWs for pals of disabled in scam', *Sun*, thesun.co.uk, 19 June 2011.

39 Neil Tweedie, 'The car scam that will drive you crackers: As the Lottery con grandmother is given this £20,000 car, we reveal how thousands are driving off in brand new vehicles paid for by YOU', *Daily Mail*, dailymail.co.uk, 11 May 2016.

40 Dan Bloom, 'Cruel Tory benefit shake-up has forced 75,000 disabled people to give up their adapted cars', *Daily Mirror*, mirror.co.uk, 5 March 2018.

41 Jon Vale, 'Almost 80% of people on disability benefits "have seen health worsen since introduction of Tories' new system"', *Independent*, 13 September 2017.

42 Ibid.

43 Patrick Butler, 'Motability needs a new road map for managing finances, MPs say', *Guardian*, theguardian.com, 21 May 2018.

44 Simon Murphy and Patrick Butler, 'Motability firm boss quits after news of £2.2m bonus', *Guardian*, theguardian.com, 7 December 2018.

45 John Pring, 'Tory peer attacks McVey over "litany of inaccuracies" on Motability', *Disability News Service*, disabilitynewsservice.com, 22 February 2018.

46 Toby Helm, 'Disabled people lose legal aid in 99% of benefits disputes', *Observer*, theguardian.com, 14 April 2018.

47 YouGov for Back Up, 'Back Up wheelchair survey 2017', backuptrust.org. uk, 14 November 2017.

48 Emily Dugan and Tom Phillips, 'How your chances of getting an NHS wheelchair vary wildly depending on where you live', *BuzzFeed*, buzzfeed. com, 1 August 2017.

49 Ibid.

50 Ibid.

51 Sharon Brennon, ' "Alarming" figures show thousands still waiting too long for wheelchairs', *Health Service Journal*, hsj.co.uk, 14 August 2018.

52 Denis Campbell, 'Millions of patients denied use of a wheelchair', *Guardian*, theguardian.com, 27 July 2018.

53 Press Association, 'Disabled patients "relying on crowdfunding" for wheel-chairs', theguardian.com, 27 June 2017.

54 Access and Mobility Professional, 'Wheelchair-user woes revealed in new report calling for "urgent innovation" ', accessandmobilityprofessional.com, 30 April 2018.

55 Frances Ryan, 'Need a wheelchair? Pay for it yourself', *Guardian*, theguard-ian.com, 19 July 2017.

4 *Housing*

1 EHRC, 'Housing and disabled people: Britain's hidden crisis', equalityhu-manrights.com, 11 May 2018.

2 LSE, '1.8 million disabled people struggling to find accessible housing', lse. ac.uk, 29 July 2016.

3 Leonard Cheshire, 'No place like home', leonardcheshire.org, 1 December 2014.

4 EHRC, 'Housing and disabled people: Britain's hidden crisis', equalityhu-manrights.com, 11 May 2018.

5 James Meikle, 'People with disabilities treated like second-class citizens, says watchdog', *Guardian*, theguardian.com, 19 July 2016.

6 EHRC, 'Housing and disabled people'.

7 Robert Booth, 'Builders criticised for lobbying against accessible homes', *Guardian*, theguardian.com, 28 November 2018.

8 Ibid.

9 Ibid.

10 Leonard Cheshire, 'The long wait for a home', Leonardcheshire.org.uk, 19 April 2015.

11 EHRC, 'Equality Commission calls for end to Scotland's hidden disability housing crisis', equalityhumanrights.com, 11 May 2018.

12 John Pring, 'Concerns over Green Paper's "chilling' chilling" failure to address accessible housing crisis', *Disability News Service*, disabilitynewsservice.com, 16 August 2018.

13 EHRC, 'Housing and disabled people: Britain's hidden crisis', equalityhumanrights.com, 11 May 2018.

14 Leonard Cheshire, 'The real cost of the lack of disabled-friendly homes', 1 February 2014.

15 Mind, 'Four in five people with mental health problems say their housing has made their mental health worse', mind.org.uk, 3 May 2018.

16 LSE, '1.8 million disabled people struggling to find accessible housing', lse.ac.uk, 29 July 2016.

17 Resolution Foundation, 'Up to a third of millennials face renting from cradle to grave', resolutionfoundation.org, 17 April 2018.

18 National Housing Federation, 'Baby boomers hit by "shattering impact" of housing crisis', housing.org.uk, 30 April 2018.

19 Toby Helm and Jonah Ramchandan, 'Give Britain's young homebuyers state loans for deposits, urges report', *Observer*, theguardian.com, 29 July 2018.

20 National Housing Federation, 'No DSS: Five leading letting agents risk breaking the law', www.housing.org.uk, 22 August 2018.

21 Helen Pidd, 'Landlords "unwilling" to rent to universal credit recipients', *Guardian*, theguardian.com, 24 December 2017.

22 National Housing Federation, 'Baby boomers hit by "shattering impact" of housing crisis', housing.org.uk, 30 April 2018.

23 Benjamin Kentish, 'Number of government-funded social homes falls by 97% since Conservatives took office', *Independent*, independent.co.uk, 20 June 2018.

24 Robert Booth, 'England needs 3m new social homes by 2040, says cross-party report', *Guardian,* theguardian.com, 8 January 2019.

25 Press Association, 'More than 1m families waiting for social housing in England', *Guardian,* theguardian.com, 9 June 2018.

26 BBC Media Centre, 'No place to call home', bbc.co.uk, 19 October 2016.

27 Jamie Doward, 'Housing crisis drives more than 1m private tenants deeper into poverty', *Observer*, theguardian.com, 22 September 2018.

28 Shelter, 'More than 300,000 people in Britain homeless today', shelter.org.uk, 8 November 2017.

29 Ibid.

30 National Audit Office, 'Homelessness', nao.org, 13 September 2017.

31 Frances Perraudin and Niamh McIntryre, 'Councils "ripped off" by private landlords, experts warn', *Guardian,* theguardian.com, 1 January 2019.

32 Bill Davies, 'In filthy, dangerous accommodation, Britain's hidden homeless are suffering', *Guardian*, theguardian.com, 20 January 2016.

33 Becky Snow, 'Here's the real story of homelessness and domestic abuse that the statistics hide', *Guardian*, theguardian.com, 15 December 2017.

34 George Osborne, 'George Osborne's speech to the Conservative conference: Full text', *New Statesman*, newstatesman.com, 8 October 2012.

35 John Pring, 'Lower benefit cap sees income slashed for more than 10,000 disabled people', *Disability News Service*, disabilitynewsservice.com, 11 May 2017.

36 Department for Work and Pensions, 'Equality impact assessment for benefit cap', www.gov.uk, 23 July 2012.

37 Rajeev Syal, '"Bedroom tax" will hit single parents and disabled people hardest', *Guardian*, theguardian.com, 4 March 2013.

38 EHRC, 'Is Britain fairer?', equalityhumanrights.com, 25 October 2018.

39 May Bulman, 'More than 57,000 people hit by bedroom tax fall behind on rent, Government report reveals', *Independent*, independent.co.uk, 22 July 2016.

40 Steven Swinford, 'Most people think "bedroom tax" is fair, poll finds', *Daily Telegraph*, telegraph.co.uk, 8 November 2013.

41 Frances Ryan, '"Bedroom tax" puts added burden on disabled people', *Guardian*, theguardian.com, 16 July 2013.

42 Carers UK, 'Bedroom tax: Carers facing debt, eviction and food poverty', carersuk.org, 9 July 2013.

43 Ros Wynne Jones and Dan Bloom, 'Tories finally make legal changes to the Bedroom Tax after humiliating court defeat', *Daily Mirror*, mirror.co.uk, 3 March 2017.

44 Emily Dugan, '"Big lie" behind the bedroom tax: Families trapped with nowhere to move face penalty for having spare room', *Independent*, independent.co.uk, 5 August 2013.

45 Crisis, 'More than 24,000 people facing Christmas sleeping rough or in cars, trains, buses and tents', crisis.org.uk, 14 December 2018.

46 National Audit Office, 'Homelessness', nao.org.uk, 13 September 2017.

47 Robert Booth, 'Rise in homelessness not result of our policies, says housing secretary', *Guardian,* theguardian.com, 18 December 2018; Lizzie Dearden, 'Conservative austerity policies may have driven homelessness rise, housing secretary admits', *Independent,* independent.co.uk, 24 December 2018

48 Patrick Butler, 'Welfare reforms are main cause of homelessness in England, study finds', *Guardian*, theguardian.com, 4 February 2015.

49 Patrick Butler, 'Families with stable jobs at risk of homelessness in England, report finds', *Guardian*, theguardian.com, 15 December 2017.

50 St Mungo's, 'Stop the scandal: The case for action on mental health and rough sleeping', mungos.org, November 2016.

51 Ibid.

52 Patrick Greenfield et al., 'At least 440 homeless people died in UK in past year, study shows', *Guardian,* theguardian.com, 8 October 2018.

53 Patrick Greenfield and Sarah Marsh, 'Deaths of UK homeless people more than double in five years', *Guardian,* theguardian.com, 11 April 2018.

54 Sarah Marsh and Patrick Greenfield, 'Deaths of mentally ill rough sleepers in London rise sharply', *Guardian*, theguardian.com, 19 June 2018.

55 Ibid.

56 Mark Lister, 'Homeless wheelchair-bound mum found dead in doorway of House of Fraser store', *Daily Mirror*, mirror.co.uk, 7 March 2019.

57 Good4You, 'Social exclusion, disability and homelessness', good4you.org. uk, no date 2018.

58 Homeless Link, 'Over half of homeless people suffer from chronic pain', homeless.org.uk, 10 September 2018.

59 Ibid.

60 Ibid.

61 Crisis, 'Turned away', crisis.org.uk, 15 October 2014.

62 Crisis, 'Rough sleeping set to rise by three quarters in next decade as report reveals scale of acute homelessness in Britain', crisis.org.uk, 10 August 2017.

63 Toby Helm, 'Housing crisis threatens a million families with eviction by 2020', *Observer*, theguardian.com, 24 June 2017.

64 National Audit Office, 'Rolling out Universal Credit', nao.org.uk, 15 June 2018.

65 Patrick Butler, 'Disabled people could slip through net in universal credit move, says charity', *Guardian*, theguardian.com, 5 July 2018.

5 *Women*

1 Patrick Butler, 'Government to review 1.6m disability benefit claims after U-turn', *Guardian*, theguardian.com, 29 January 2018.

2 Mikey Smith, 'Universal Credit is driving women to prostitution says MP Frank Field in astonishing plea to Esther McVey', *Daily Mirror*, mirror. co.uk, 15 October 2018.

3 Lizzy Buchan, 'TUC leaders reject call to decriminalise prostitution', *Independent*, independent.co.uk, 13 September 2017.

4 Changing Lives, 'The type of girl that would do that', changing-lives.org. uk, 17 October 2016.

5 *Star*, 'Sheffield women being forced into prostitution by benefit cuts', thestar.co.uk, 2 November 2016.

6 Ibid.

7 Ibid.

8 Ian Silvera, 'Fawcett Society: Financial crisis pushed 826,000 women into low paid work', *International Business Times*, ibtimes.co.uk, 18 August 2014.

9 Ibid.

10 Women's Budget Group, 'The female face of poverty', wbg.org.uk, 18 July 2018.

11 Ibid

12 SafeLives, SafeLives briefing to Frances Ryan, 2018.

13 Women's Aid, 'Support for disabled women', womensaid.org.uk, no date 2014.

14 Refuge, Refuge briefing to Frances Ryan, 2018.

15 SafeLives, 'Disability and domestic violence', safelives.org.uk, 22 November 2016.

16 Ibid.

17 SafeLives, 'Disabled survivors too: Disabled people and domestic abuse', safelives.org.uk, March 2017.

18 University of Kent, 'Don't put up with it: Domestic violence and women with learning disabilities', kent.ac.uk, 26 January 2015.

19 SafeLives, 'Disabled survivors too: Disabled people and domestic abuse', safelives.org.uk, March 2017.

20 BBC News, 'Why disabled women can't access all refuges', bbc.co.uk, 28 November 2018.

21 Jamie Grierson, 'Council funding for women's refuges cut by nearly £7m since 2010', *Guardian*, theguardian.com, 23 March 2018.

22 Lizzy Buchan, 'Women's refuge budgets slashed by nearly a quarter over past seven years', *Independent,* independent.co.uk, 17 October 2017.

23 Alexandra Topping, 'Universal Credit is backward step in tackling domestic abuse, MPs warn', *Guardian*, theguardian.com, 22 October 2018.

24 Tom Macleod, 'Domestic violence victims "sleeping rough" after refuges closed', *Sky News*, news.sky.com, 21 October 2017.

25 Ibid. Peter Walker and Kevin Rawlinson, 'Universal credit to be paid to main carer in attempt to help women', *Guardian*, theguardian.com, 11 January 2019.

26 *Full Fact*, 'Are more children being taken from their families?' fullfact.org, 29 March 2018.

27 Sandra Laville, 'Children unnecessarily removed from parents, report claims', *Guardian*, theguardian.com, 18 January 2017.

28 Ibid.

29 Legal Action for Women, 'Suffer the little children and their mothers: A dossier on the unjust separation of children from their mothers', legalactionforwomen.net, 18 January 2017.

30 Sandra Laville, 'Children unnecessarily removed from parents, report claims', *Guardian*, theguardian.com, 18 January 2017.

31 Nuffield Foundation, 'Inequalities in child welfare intervention rates', nuffieldfoundation.org, no date 2017.

32 Patrick Butler, 'Austerity policy blamed for record numbers of children taken into care', *Guardian*, theguardian.com, 11 October 2017.

33 Ibid.

34 Action for Children, 'Budgets for children's early help services suffer £743 million funding drop in five years, figures show', actionforchildren.org.uk, 27 September 2018.

35 Frances Perraudin and Niamh McIntyre, 'Rise in children taken into care pushes 88% of councils over budget', *Guardian,* theguardian.com, 8 January 2019.

36 Engender, 'Our bodies, our rights: Identifying and removing barriers to disabled women's reproductive rights in Scotland', engender.org.uk, 6 November 2018.

37 Sisters of Frida, 'Disabled women: Facts and stats', sisofrida.org, no date 2017.

38 UK Women's Budget Group, 'Disabled women and austerity', wbg.org.uk, 22 October 2018.

39 Ibid.

40 Victoria Brignell, 'The eugenics movement Britain wants to forget', *New Statesman*, newstatesman.com, 9 December 2010.

41 Ibid.

42 Kyoko Hasegawa, 'Lifetimes of pain: Victims of Japan's forced sterilization program hope for justice, or at least an apology', *Japan Times*, japantimes.co.jp, 20 April 2018.

43 Bridie Jabour, 'UN examines Australia's forced sterilisation of women with disabilities', *Guardian Australia*, theguardian.com, 10 November 2015.

44 Disability Research on Independent Living and Learning (Drill), the University of Bedfordshire and Ginger Giraffe, 'Re-imagining social care services in co-production with disabled parents and professionals', 26 September 2018.

45 Sally Williams, 'Who cares? Meet the children who juggle school with looking after their parents', *Daily Telegraph*, telegraph.co.uk, 23 January 2016.

46 Dave Howard, 'Number of child carers "four times previous estimate"', BBC News, bbc.co.uk, 16 November 2010.

47 BBC News, 'Being a young carer', bbc.co.uk, 14 September 2018.

48 Ibid.

49 Ben Quinn, 'Thousands of children as young as five act as family carers, figures show', *Guardian*, theguardian.com, 16 May 2013.

50 May Bulman, 'Number of young carers in UK soars by 10,000 in four years, figures show', *Independent*, independent.co.uk, 28 January 2018.

51 Ibid.

52 Children's Society, 'Hidden from view: The experiences of young carers in England', childrenssociety.org.uk, May 2013.

53 BBC News, 'Being a young carer', 2018.

54 May Bulman, 'Number of young carers in UK soars by 10,000 in four years, figures show', *Independent*, independent.co.uk, 28 January 2018.

55 Patrick Butler, 'Four out five young carers receive no council support, says study', *Guardian*, theguardian.com, 27 December 2016.

56 Ibid.

57 Ibid.

58 Ibid.

59 *Somerset County Gazette*, 'Somerset County Council approves millions in cuts – but those to young carers' services have been delayed', somersetcountygazette.co.uk, 12 September 2018.

6 Children

1 *Daily Mirror*, 'Shame of ConDem cuts', 16 April 2014.

2 Andrew Brown, 'Perhaps it doesn't matter if the Daily Mirror's weeping child is a lie', *Guardian*, theguardian.com, 16 April 2014.

3 Heather Stewart and Richard Partington, 'Poorest families to lose out on £210 a year owing to benefits cap', *Guardian*, theguardian.com, 13 October 2018.

4 Contact, analysis for Frances Ryan, 2018.

5 Contact, 'Counting the costs', contact.org.uk, 5 December 2018.

6 Joseph Rowntree Foundation, analysis for Frances Ryan, 2018.

7 Contact, 'Counting the costs', contact.org.uk, 5 December 2018.

8 Ibid.

9 Ibid.

10 EHRC, 'Being disabled in Britain: A journey less equal', equalityhumanrights.com, 3c April 2017.

11 Ibid.

12 Richard Adams, 'Hundreds of children's playgrounds in England close due to cuts', *Guardian*, theguardian.com, 13 April 2017.

13 Mark Blunden, 'The council playground in London that costs £20 a time', *Evening Standard*, standard.co.uk, 20 January 2014.

14 National Youth Agency, 'Cuts watch: Policy update on local authority cuts to youth services', nya.org.uk, 15 December 2014.

15 Patrick Butler '1,000 Sure Start children's centres may have shut since 2010', *Guardian*, theguardian.com, 5 April 2018.

16 Letters, 'In austerity Britain, people need parks', *Guardian*, theguardian. com, 25 December 2017.

17 Disabled Children's Partnership, 'The case for a disabled child's fund', disabledchildrenspartnership.org.uk, 16 July 2018.

18 Ibid.

19 National Children's Bureau, 'Put children and young people at the heart of Government spending', ncb.org.uk, 17 October 2018.

20 Every Disabled Child Matters, 'Short breaks in 2015: An uncertain future', contact.org, 25 September 2015.

21 Ibid.

22 Contact, 'Caring more than most', contact.org.uk, 29 November 2017.

23 Alicia Clegg, 'Respite care: Families at breaking point as councils slash funds', *Guardian*, theguardian.com, 22 August 2018.

24 Contact, 'School transport inquiry', contact.org.uk, September 2017.

25 Carers UK, 'Carers call for more support as new figures reveal worrying impact of caring', carersuk.org, 19 May 2015.

26 Amy Walker, 'Single mum's heartbreaking suicide note to parents after struggling to care for her wheelchair-bound daughter', *Daily Mirror*, mirror. co.uk, 26 October 2018.

27 Jenny Morris, *Pride against Prejudice*, Women's Press Ltd, 1991.

28 Sally Weale, '£3.5bn cut for school buildings leaves pupils in crumbling classrooms – Labour', *Guardian*, theguardian.com, 26 October 2018.

29 Mark Ellis, 'Head teachers warn children with disabilities are hit hardest by Tory austerity agenda', *Daily Mirror*, mirror.co.uk, 3 May 2018.

30 National Deaf Children's Society, 'New data shows councils cutting £4million of support for deaf children', ndcs.org.uk, 15 May 2018.

31 Michael Savage, 'Children in special needs education face £1.6bn cash shortfall', *Observer*, theguardian.com, 16 December 2018.

32 Sally Weale and Niamh McIntyre, 'Special needs pupils being failed by system "on verge of crisis"', *Guardian*, theguardian.com, 22 October 2018.

33 Department for Education, 'Special educational needs in England: January 2018', gov.uk, 26 July 2018.

34 Patrick Butler, 'UN panel criticises UK failure to uphold disabled people's rights', *Guardian*, theguardian.com, 31 August 2017.

35 Tania Tirraoro, 'Exclusions 2018: Children with SEND six times more likely to be excluded', *Special Needs Jungle*, specialneedsjungle.com, 20 July 2018.

36 Gary Younge, 'The British state has given up on the children who need it most', theguardian.com, 16 November 2018.

37 National Education Union, 'Vulnerable special needs pupils at risk of exclusion due to funding cuts – NEU survey', neu.org.uk, 13 April 2018.

38 Chaminda Jayanetti and Michael Savage, '"Devastating" cuts hit special educational needs', *Observer,* theguardian.com, 10 November 2018.

39 Sally Weale, 'Families take Surrey council to court over special needs funding', *Guardian*, theguardian.com, 2 October 2018.

40 Tania Tirraoro, 'SEND system in crisis, say headteachers', *Special Needs Jungle*, specialneedsjungle.com, 5 September 2018.

41 Richard Adams, 'Special needs funding at crisis point, say school leaders', *Guardian*, theguardian.com, 5 September 2018.

42 Branwen Jeffreys, 'Horrendous meltdowns: Why I home-educate my daughter', BBC News, bbc.co.uk, 27 November 2017.

43 Sally Weale and Niamh McIntyre, 'Thousands of children with special needs excluded from schools', *Guardian*, theguardian.com, 23 October 2018.

44 Sally Weale, 'Ofsted condemns "disjointed" special educational needs provision', *Guardian*, theguardian.com, 4 December 2018.

45 Ibid.

46 Ibid.

47 Joseph Rowntree Foundation, 'Special educational needs and their links to poverty,' jrf.org.uk, 26 February 2016.

48 Caroline Wheeler, 'General Election 2017: Theresa May vows to "rip up" Mental Health Act', *Daily Express*, express.co.uk, 7 May 2017.

49 Katie Forster, 'Third of NHS children's mental health services "face cuts or closure"', *Independent,* independent.co.uk, 22 May 2017.

50 Denis Campbell, 'Children waiting up to 18 months for mental health treatment – CQC', *Guardian*, theguardian.com, 20 October 2017.

51 Richard Adams, 'Tens of thousands of children in England rejected for mental health treatment', *Guardian*, theguardian.com, 7 October 2017.

52 Frances Ryan, 'When the state abandons suicidal children, something has gone badly wrong', *Guardian*, theguardian.com, 26 October 2018.

53 Sarah Ward and Michael Young, 'Council ordered to reverse special needs

cuts in landmark High Court case', *Independent*, independent.co.uk, 6 August 2018.
54 RNIB, 'Parents force Hackney Council to reverse plans', rnib.org.uk, 9 March 2018.

Conclusion

1 Patrick Butler, 'Exclusive: universal credit linked to suicide risk, says study', *Guardian*, theguardian.com, 15 November 2018.
2 Patrick Butler, 'UK survey finds huge support for ending austerity', *Guardian*, theguardian.com, 28 June 2017.
3 Women's Budget Group, 'Government must take urgent action on poverty', wbg.org.uk, 16 November 2018.

Afterword

1 Georgina Hayes, 'Housing charities and food banks report spike in donations after Tory win', *Guardian*, 14 December 2019.
2 Sarah Boseley, 'Austerity blamed for life expectancy stalling for first time in century', *Guardian*, 25 February 2020.
3 BBC News, 'Poorest women's life expectancy declines, finds report,' bbc.co.uk, 25 February 2020.
4 Patrick Butler, 'Universal credit could "steamroll vulnerable into poverty"', *Guardian*, 11 February 2020.
5 L. O'Carroll, P. Walker, L. Brooks, 'UK to close door to non-english speakers and unskilled workers', *Guardian*, 11 February 2020.
6 Rowena Mason, 'Boris Johnson adviser quits over race and eugenics controversy', *Guardian*, 17 February 2020.
7 Frances Ryan, 'DWP accused of offering disabled people "take it of leave it benefits"', *Guardian*, 2 March 2020.
8 Patrick Butler, 'Disabled man starved to death after DWP stopped his benefits', *Guardian*, 28 January 2020.
9 Patrick Butler and Peter Walker, 'UK's emergency coronavirus bill "will put vulnerable at risk"', *Guardian*, 23 March 2020.
10 Patrick Butler, 'Benefits changes leave disabled people facing poverty, charities warned, *Guardian*, 30 March 2020.
11 Patrick Butler, 'Covid 19 Mutual Aid: how to help vulnerable people around you', *Guardian*, 16 March 2020.

12 Robert Booth and Kevin Rawlinson, '950,000 apply for universal credit in two weeks of UK lockdown', *Guardian*, 1 April 2020.
13 Peter C. Baker, ' "P. C. "We can't go back to normal": how will coronavirus change the world?', *Guardian*, 31 March, 2020.

Help and Resources

Advice Local
A website which helps you find advice services in your area for support with benefits, work, money and housing. https://advicelocal.uk. It also helps you find a local adviser on your rights. https://advicelocal.uk/find-an-adviser.

Benefits and Work
A website run by former welfare rights advisers providing information on how to claim and retain benefits. https://www.benefitsandwork.co.uk.

C-App
A website providing guidance for people applying for the out-of-work sickness benefit Employment and Support Allowance. http://www.c-app.org.uk.

CASCAIDr

A specialist advice charity aimed at helping people get their full legal rights from the social care system. http://www.cascaidr.org.uk/about-us.

Citizens Advice

A nationwide service providing information and advice for benefit claims and appeals. https://www.citizensadvice.org.uk/benefits/sick-or-disabled-people-and-carers.

Disability Grants

A website helping disabled people find grants towards the extra costs of disability. http://www.disability-grants.org.

Disability Law Service

A charity providing free legal advice and representation for disabled people. https://dls.org.uk. Contact them on advice@dls.org.uk or 0207 791 9800.

Disability Rights UK

A disabled-person-led website that provides support in a range of areas, including independent living, career opportunities and tackling hate crime. https://www.disabilityright-suk.org/how-we-can-help.

Equality Advisory Service

A helpline assisting people on issues relating to equality and human rights (equipped to assist people with a learning disability or who are Deaf). http://www.equalityadvisoryservice.com. Contact them on Freephone 0808 800 0082 or textphone 0808 800 0084.

Fightback4Justice
A non-profit legal advice group offering nationwide support for benefit claims and appeals. http://www.fightback4justice.co.uk.

IPSEA
A charity providing free legal advice in England to help children with special educational needs and disabilities (SEND) get the right education. http://www.ipsea.org.uk.

Law for Life and Advice Now
A charity securing access to justice, including free self-help guides and tools to help people challenge benefit decisions. https://www.lawforlife.org.uk.

Pip Info
An online guide to Personal Independence Payments, as well as relevant case law. http://pipinfo.net.

Samaritans
A charity providing support for anyone in emotional distress, open twenty-four hours a day, 365 days a year. Contact them on Freephone 116 123 or email jo@samaritans.org (UK) jo@samaritans.ie (ROI).

Turn2Us
A national charity helping people in financial hardship to gain access to welfare benefits, charitable grants and support services. https://www.turn2us.org.uk/About-Us/Contact-us.

Z2K

A London-based charity providing support including free legal representation and helping secure tenancies for single homeless people. https://www.z2k.org.

Index

attention deficit hyperactivity disorder (ADHD), 65, 67, 158
Adult Social Services, 98, 159, 160
All Work Test, 48
Alston, Philip, 191
Amazon, 103
Amnesty International, 69
ASLEF, 141
Asperger's Syndrome, 16
Association of Child Psychotherapists, 187
Association of Directors of Children's Services (ADCS) 155
Atos, 49, 52, 53
Atos Miracles, 53
austerity, 3, 5, 8, 9, 10, 12, 16, 18, 21, 22, 24, 26, 28, 34, 40, 41, 54, 68, 70, 74, 75, 81, 91, 94, 98, 123, 127, 128, 130, 140, 141, 142, 144, 151, 155, 158, 165, 169, 171, 172, 178, 179, 180, 182, 192, 193, 194, 195, 198
autism, 54, 56, 57, 64, 158, 159, 181, 185, 187

Barnardo's, 166

Bedroom Tax, 12, 18, 22, 32, 124, 125, 126, 127, 135
Benefit Street, 26, 40
Betts, Mike, 96
Beveridge, Sir William, 46
Beverley Lewis House, 148
Big Issue, 130
Big Society, 80
Blair, Tony, 48
Bond, Lawrence, 51
Bureau of Investigative Journalism (BIJ), 130, 151
Brexit, 9, 80, 192, 198, 199
Brignell, Victoria, 83
British Medical Association (BMA), 102
British Red Cross, 101
British Sign Language (BSL), 58, 146, 150, 153
Brokenshire, James, 110, 127
Burnip, Linda, 86
Burns, Sandra, 51
BuzzFeed, 99, 211

Cameron, David, 2, 3, 11, 16, 80, 123,

124, 128, 169
Child and Adolescent Mental Health Services (CAMHS) 187
Care Act, 85, 167
Care and Support Alliance (CSA), 78, 89
Centre for Welfare Reform, 3, 23
clinical commissioning group (CCG), 86, 174
Changing Lives, 141, 142, 214
Child Welfare Inequality project, 154
Church, Archibald, 157
Church Action on Poverty, 35
Churchill, Winston, 157
Crichton-Brown, Sir James, 157
Citizens Advice, 33, 70, 163
Clapson, David, 39, 43
Clifford, Ellen, 161
coalition government, 3, 11, 26, 29, 39, 42, 48, 68, 73, 123, 127, 195
Comic Relief, 144
Community Care (Direct Payments) Act, 85
community care grants, 34
ComRes, 103
Conservative Party, 3, 5, 62, 193
chronic obstructive pulmonary dis ease (COPD), 92, 98
crisis loans, 34, 35
Crohn's disease, 73, 75

Davies, Philip, 62
DeafHope, 146, 153
Demos, 23, 43, 44
Department for Communities and Local Government (DCLG), 129
Department for Work and Pensions (DWP), 21, 42, 43, 45, 50, 82, 145, 153
Dinenage, Caroline, 167
disabled facilities grants (DFGs), 109
Disability Discrimination Act (DDA), 25, 64
Disability Benefits Consortium, 18

Disability Discrimination Act, 25, 64, 67
Disability Employment Act, 24
Disability Law Service, 222
Disability Living Allowance (DLA), 17, 18, 26, 27, 69, 93, 94, 134
Disability Research on Independent Living and Learning (Drill), 160
Disabled People Against Cuts (DPAC), 66, 86
Disabled Persons Act, 84
Driver, Amy, 40
Duncan Smith, Iain, 4, 26, 28, 47, 62

Education Policy Institute (EPI), 187
Employment Act, 24, 54
Employment and Support Allowance (ESA), 17, 138, 146
Equality and Human Rights Com mission (EHRC), 24, 61, 62, 87, 109, 110, 111
Equality Act, 64, 82, 124
Equality Commission, 211
Eugenics Education Society, 157
European Social Fund, 57
Every Disabled Child Matters, 218

Fawcett Society, 144, 215
fibromyalgia, 6, 49, 73, 98, 117
Field, Frank, 61
Fightback4Justice, 96, 223
Fitzpatrick, Suzanne, 21
Freedom of Information Act, 151
Freeman, George, 30
Freud, Lord David, 61

GMB, 64, 78
Greater Manchester Law Centre (GMLC), 70
Good4you, 131, 214
Great Ormond Street Hospital, 173
Greater Manchester Law Centre, 70
Guild of the Brave Poor Things, 15

Hammond, Philip, 61
Harrison Neves, Victoria, 152
Hawking, Stephen, 41, 50, 100
Home Builders Federation (HBF), 109
Health Service Journal, 100
Heath, Edward, 47
Heriot-Watt University, 20
Home Affairs Select Committee, 152
Homeless Reduction Act, 135
Housing and Finance Institute, 113

Incapacity Benefit (IB), 48
Independent Living Fund (ILF), 81, 82
Inclusion London, 161
Institute for Public Policy Research (IPPR), 120
Invalidity Benefit, 47, 48
Ipsos Mori, 125

Jimbob, 5, 6, 7
JobCentre, 33, 35, 39, 40, 50, 51, 56, 57, 58, 141, 142
Jobseeker's Allowance (JSA), 34, 35, 39, 43
Joseph Rowntree Foundation (JRF), 14, 15, 20, 127, 170, 185
JustGiving, 103

Kavanagh, Jane, 178
Kickstarter, 103

Labour Party, 42, 48, 55, 123, 126, 172, 193
Legal Action for Women, 154, 215
Leonard Cheshire, vii, 52, 56, 63, 77, 78, 107, 110, 111
Lewes Council, 118
Local Government Association (LGA), 76, 79, 155, 180
local housing allowance (LHA), 114, 123
Lifetime Homes standard, 108
Living Wage Foundation, 17

London Olympics, 2
London Paralympics, 2
London Plan, 108
Louis Vuitton, 133, 135, 136
London School of Economics (LSE), 46, 107
lupus, 73

Magna Carta, 84
Major, John, 48
Maximus, 49, 53
May, Theresa, 12, 30, 55, 76, 82, 123, 187, 193
McIntyre, Laura, 142
McVey, Esther, 30, 45, 96
Myalgic Encephalomyelitis (ME), 140
Mencap, 29
Mental Health Act, 219
Mental Incapacity Act, 83
Metcalf, David, 51
Mind, 17, 46, 100, 111, 135, 212
Ministry of Justice (MoJ), 69
Morris, Jenny, 179
Motability Scheme, 93, 94, 96, 104
multiple sclerosis (MS), 11, 89
MS Society, 89

Nascot Lawn, 174, 175, 177
National Association of Head Teachers (NAHT), 180, 183
National Audit Office (NAO), 46, 50, 53, 96, 118, 127, 135
National Deaf Children's Society (NDCS), 180
National Education Union (NEU), 182
National Housing Federation (NHF), 114, 115
National Institute of Economic and Social Research (NIESR), 52
National Insurance Act, 25, 47
National Landlords Association (NLA), 114
Nationwide Foundation, 117

New Labour, 15, 48, 55
New Policy Institute (NPI), 20
NHS England, 99
Nuffield Foundation, 216

Office of National Statistics (ONS), 59
Ofsted, 184, 219
Opportunities Project, 142
Osborne, George, 3, 75, 123, 170, 198

Papworth Trust, 63, 107, 125
Parkinson's disease, 14, 23, 46
Persimmon, 109
Personal Independence Payment
    (PIP), 26, 27, 69, 93, 94, 95, 138, 145
Peverely, Phil Dr, 41
Poor Law, 15
Portes, Jonathan, 52
Priestley, Mark, 54
Public Health England, 148
Public Interest Research Unit (PIRU),
    66, 67
Public Service Excellence, 79

RADAR, 84, 140
Refuge, vii, 147, 148, 149, 150, 151,
    152, 215
Resolution Foundation, 113, 170, 212
Royal Association for Disability
    Rights (RADAR), 84
Royal Commission on the Care and
    Control of the Feeble-Minded, 157
Royal National Institute of Blind
    People (RNIB), 29

SafeLives, 147, 148
Salter, Tim, 52
Samaritans, 223
sanctions, 42, 43, 44, 45, 46, 117, 127,
    141, 142, 169
Scottish Welfare Fund, 35
Seebohm, Laura, 142
Shah, Sonali, 54
Sheffield Working Women, 142

Shelter, 14, 105, 114, 116, 118, 134,
    135
Sisters of Frida, 156
Sisters Uncut, 122
Social Metrics Commission, 15
Somerset County Council, 168
special educational needs and disabili-
    ties (SEND), 180, 182, 183, 184, 189
St Mungo's, 128, 130, 213
Sure Start, 155, 172, 218

Thatcher, Margaret, 28
Thompson, Gail, 40
Tilda Goldberg Centre for Social
    Work and Social Care, 160
Tizard Centre, 149
Toyota Mobility Foundation, 103
Trussell Trust, 36

UK Women's Budget Group, 156
University College London (UCL), 91
University of Bedfordshire, 160,
University of Kent, 149
University of Liverpool, 51
University of Manchester, 60
University of Oxford, 36
University of York, 43

West Sussex County Council, 36
Whizz-kidz, 102
Winterbourne View, 90, 91
Without Nascot Lawn, 177
Women's Budget Group, 92, 145, 156
Wood, Claudia, 23
Work Capability Assessment (WCA),
    47, 48, 49, 50
Work and Health Programme, 57
Work and Pensions Committee, 27,
    61, 141
Work Choice, 57
Work Programme, 57